HEAL YOUR AURA

FINDING TRUE LOVE BY GENERATING A POSITIVE ENERGY FIELD

MURIEL MACFARLANE

CITADEL PRESS
KENSINGTON PUBLISHING CORP.
www.kensingtonbooks.com

CITADEL PRESS books are published by

Kensington Publishing Corp.
850 Third Avenue
New York, NY 10022

All Kensington titles, imprints, and distributed lines are available at special quantity discounts for bulk purchases for sales promotions, premiums, fund raising, educational, or institutional use. Special book excerpts or customized printings can also be created to fit specific needs. For details, write or phone the office of the Kensington special sales manager: Kensington Publishing Corp., 850 Third Avenue, New York, NY 10022, attn: Special Sales Department, phone 1-800-221-2647.

Kensington and the K logo Reg. U.S. Pat. & TM Office
Citadel Press is a trademark of Kensington Publishing Corp.

First printing 2000

10 9 8 7 6 5 4 3 2 1

Printed in the United States of America

Library of Congress Cataloging-in-Publication Data

MacFarlane, Muriel
    Heal Your aura : finding true love by generating a positive energy field / Muriel MacFarlane.
        p.   cm.
    "A Citadel Press book."
    Includes bibliographical references and index.
    ISBN 0-8065-2132-5 (pbk.)
    1. Aura. 2. Love—Miscellanea. 3. Mate selection—Miscellania.
I. Title.
    BF1389.A8M23   1999
    133.8'92—dc21   99-40383
                                                CIP

This book is dedicated to the
Power of the Universe,
which can change your life.

CONTENTS

ACKNOWLEDGMENTS

I want to acknowledge the kindness of friends, Sue Kovach, Wayne Grover, Catharine Rambeau, Martha Moffett, and Dorothy Duffy, who have been generous with their time and talent. I wish to thank my agent, Noah Lukeman, for his support, kind thoughts, words, and gentle manner, and my editor, Hillel Black at Carol Publishing, whom I have never met but whose aura I have sensed.

I would like to thank all those whose aura has brushed against or touched mine during our lifetimes.

In particular I would like to thank those who have allowed me to see into some small part of their worlds and who have demonstrated that they can nurture friends and families, support others, and grow in emotional and spiritual stature as they look for peace and love in their own lives, while they energized their chakras and brightened their auras.

I also want to thank all those people who participated in developing the quizzes and the tasks, who reported back about the changes that were taking place in their lives and the differences they felt as they tried to open their chakras to the energy of the universe, who concentrated on having an aura that is warm and bright, sending kindness and compassion out to the world and at the same time bringing trustworthy lovers into their worlds.

I enjoyed knowing and watching their progress throughout as the rhythms of the universe coursed through their bodies: Diana Downs, Anne Richmond, Phyllis Ross, Bette Chapparelli, Gladys Nichols, Ruth Thone, Earle and Mitzi Staley, Jim and Sheila Milne, Wainetta and Harold Coffman, Chris Fensel, Steven Krolik,

Lana Thompson, Marilyn Tucker, May Helen Hinkel, Neil Shireman, Joan McCamish, Bevely Callaway, Augusta Wynn, Kim Dillard, Barbara Alspaugh, Leslie Hartigan, Dr. E. Piscatelli, Sister Mary, and Emma Peal—and some who are now a part of the universal consciousness: Dr. Edward Downs, Carol Scott, Cleo Downs, and Dr. Haridas Chaudhuri.

HEAL YOUR AURA

1 Why Can't You Find Mr. or Ms. Right, No Matter How Hard You Try?

The men that women marry,
And why they marry them, will always be
A marvel and a mystery to the world

—Henry Wadsworth Longfellow

He's good-looking, charming, has an excellent job, and knows how to sweet-talk any woman he meets. At first, he looks like the Prince Charming that every woman has waited for and dreamed about. Your Mr. Right. Or is he?

She's beautiful, compassionate; she actually listens to you. She's interested in everything that is important to you. At first, she seems exactly like the woman of your dreams. Your Ms. Right. Or is she?

What goes wrong? If you had met each other in a singles bar or through a chance conversation struck up over folding clothes at the laundromat, then perhaps you could understand. Lots of people just looking for casual sex might hang out at such easy meeting places—people just looking for some flesh, a warm body for the night or a couple of hours, who will never have to have that terrible word they find impossible to say stick in both of their throats. Cccccccc . . . commitment.

Worse yet, you didn't pick each other up at a bar, at a wild party, or even at the laundromat. You met on the job, your Aunt Sarah introduced you, or you found each other at church or some other place, that sent a message right from the beginning you had a mutual interest or a common bond. It seems so logical that having something in common could develop into more than friendship—a relationship, a long time love affair, a marriage with children.

Everyone has a romantic dream, perhaps fostered by the movies, television, or romance novels. A dream and a hope that makes you believe in that ultimate romantic scene: You will suddenly see a stranger and your heart will race as you walk toward each other, ignoring everyone and everything else around you. And that chance meeting will be so right, so perfect, you will finally have found your soul mate, the one whom the gods intended for you. Out of all the people on the planet, the person destiny selected to be your partner for life will appear and you will both know, immediately, that it is Fate. Kismet. And you keep hoping that true love will happen just like that, someday soon.

Unfortunately, over and over again, no matter how you meet— whether through a proper introduction by people with your best interests at heart or when "lightning strikes" after you exchange glances with a stranger in a nearby car—something always seems to go wrong. Later, you look back over the months, or even years, that were wasted on a flawed relationship that ended with hurt feelings, regrets, discouragement, and a broken heart.

Disappointed and disillusioned, you move on. Sadder and perhaps a little wiser, you always hope that the next one will be the right one; you pray that someday you will find someone who is genuine, trustworthy, honest, and honorable, someone worthy of your love and total commitment.

If you ever walked through your hometown mall during any holiday such as Christmas or Easter, you have seen dozens, perhaps hundreds of couples standing in line with baby strollers and holding toddlers by the hand, waiting to have their children's picture taken with Santa or the Easter Bunny. You've seen grandparents waiting in the background with an older child, smiling fondly at the scene and then at each other. Plenty of other people have found someone to come home to, to make a home and a family with. They were able to find their Mr. or Ms. Right. They made a commitment to the future of a life together. Why can't you?

It also doesn't take much reading to realize that 60 percent of today's marriages end in divorce; single-parent homes are increasing at an astronomical rate, bringing with them all the problems that come with raising children solo; spousal violence is in the news every day; and many people are so fearful of dating that they hire private detectives to check up on even potential casual dates.

The Rules, a book written by two young women, became an instant international bestseller by providing tips on how to get a man to commit to a relationship. The huge response to that book prompted two young men to write a tongue-in-cheek response, *The Code.* Their book, however, revealed secrets of how to get what you want from women without marrying them. *The Rules* can be found in the relationship section of your local bookstore, but it is really about a honest commitment? And *The Code* is found in the humor section, but is it really funny?

Stories of relationships, long and short, ancient history or ongoing, all seem to have a point at which the people telling them realize relationships are never simple or easy to understand, particularly for the individuals involved. The hardest part may be figuring out why they happened at all and why, for some of us, the same scenario seems to occur over and over again. And finally, perhaps the most difficult question of all: What did any of us learn from these painful relationships?

Blame and self-criticism often don't help us avoid repeating our past mistakes. Laura and Trevor are good examples. Although each wanted a new relationship to turn out differently from past ones, they both found themselves in the same situations again and again. Each time they wondered what they had done wrong and how to change these patterns and finally find a good relationship, based on mutual trust and respect.

Laura

Laura had been through two long-term relationships, both of which ended badly, and she felt bitter and disappointed.

"I can understand the failure of my first marriage," she said. A truly beautiful, angelic-looking blond, with great big blue eyes fringed with luxuriant lashes, Laura leaned forward with her chin cupped in her hand as she tried to explain what had happened in her life.

"I grew up in San Diego. It's a great Navy town and there are always sailors around. I was just a kid really, almost sixteen, when I went with my girlfriend on a Saturday afternoon to the video arcade in the mall. There were lots of kids in there, kids I knew from school. We were just watching some cute guy with a pony-tail put money into one of the games when two sailors came up from behind us and asked if they could buy us a Coke. We both laughed because we had heard all the stories about sailors. We knew girls at school who had gotten involved with sailors and we all kind of looked down on them. We thought they were dumb. My parents had warned us that these guys were away from their own hometowns and we wouldn't know very much about them. They were too old for us and we needed to be careful because the very next day they might be gone.

"We were warned all the time, 'Don't get involved with any sailors.' You know, 'a girl in every port,' 'love 'em and leave 'em' stuff, but when I looked at Tim, there was something special about him. He was so strong and clean, he had big brown eyes that just seemed so warm and friendly. His uniform was spotless and his shoes were shined. Compared to the boys in the arcade with raggedy baggy jeans, scraggly hair, and basketball shirts, he looked great. Right away I thought he might be different from the rest, different from what my parents had said sailors would be like.

"I've made some very immature and foolish mistakes," Laura said, smiling sadly at her memories. "My parents didn't have a lot of money and there were lots of rules in my house. I thought my parents were overly protective. I was in such a hurry to grow up, to be out of the house and in charge of my own life. I was never a very good student. I had even tried to drop out of school several times, but my parents wouldn't let me.

"That afternoon at the mall we played video games and the sailors put their money into the machines. Tim was an excellent player and he won a great big stuffed animal, a Pooh bear, for me. When Tim and his friend asked us to walk around the mall with them, it seemed harmless enough. So we left the arcade and began strolling past all the store windows with them, daydreaming about what we would buy when we were rich and famous. That afternoon with those two sailors was wonderful, just like in a movie. These were real men, not silly dumb teenage boys, and they were interested in us! Then we went to eat and they bought us whatever we wanted. They seemed to have money just to throw around. That afternoon we laughed and laughed so much, it was like we had known them forever. We all got along just great.

"At the end of the day I had to hide the big Pooh bear at my friend's house because I couldn't take it home and explain to my parents where I had gotten it. That was just the beginning of my lying to my parents so I could see Tim. I realize now our whole relationship was based on a fabric of lies from the beginning.

"I'll make it short," Laura continued. "Within three months I was pregnant. My parents were horrified. There was no longer any argument about my dropping out of school. They didn't want to be embarrassed by having everyone see that I was pregnant. They said they couldn't take the shame, that I had dishonored and disgraced them. They could barely look at me and they wouldn't even talk to Tim. My parents were so disappointed in me, and living at home became intolerable. I couldn't discuss the baby with them; they just threw up their hands and walked away. Tim and I got married fast and everybody thought because of the baby coming, the sooner the better it would be. We were lucky to find a place to live in Navy housing. I was so homesick and lonesome there, I didn't know any other wives and I had morning sickness for months. I was so miserable, I didn't know what to do with myself. I just cried and cried all the time and I was too proud to let my parents know because I was sure they would say, 'We told you so.'

"That's when I found out that I didn't really know much of anything at all about my new husband. He wasn't twenty, as he'd told me; he was twenty-four. He also lied about his job; he was a cook, not an air traffic controller. He'd never played in a rock band, he didn't know the famous people he'd told me he knew, and he wasn't from a wealthy family in Philadelphia. Every day he lectured me about my appearance, how I needed to fix my hair and put on make-up, even if I was just sitting around the house, because his buddies might drop by and he wanted me to look good. Eight months later, when his time in the Navy was up, he took me home to a little town in Wisconsin to live with his parents. He got a job cooking in a local restaurant, which meant that he was away long hours and I was stuck with a new baby and some strangers, his parents.

When he finished work now, he wanted to go out with his buddies and he certainly didn't want to come home to a weeping wife and a crying baby. I don't want to make it sound like Tim was terrible to me because he wasn't. He told colorful stories about himself because I guess he thought it would make him seem more interesting. I can say that I pretended to be what he wanted me to be, too, because what I really wanted was to get out of my parents' house. Actually, when I think back on it, his parents were pretty kind to me. I guess they were surprised, too, to suddenly find themselves with a pregnant teenage daughter-in-law.

"I had just fallen in love with love itself—not with Tim, and certainly not with this new life that just sort of happened to me. I realize now that Tim had a vision of how he wanted life to be too: a docile wife, one he could be proud to show off to his pals, one who would have dinner on the table when he came home, a clean house, and healthy, cheerful children running to the door to throw their arms around their daddy's neck—and later, sons to play sports with.

"Three years later, still not twenty, I was so miserable that I had no choice. To get out of my unhappy situation, I had to swallow my pride and there I was, back at home with my own parents, this time with a baby and no high school diploma. I was very, very unhappy. I have to give my parents credit because by this time they had become resigned to what I had done and they didn't punish me with a lot of 'We told you so's.' But it was there unspoken all the time, and I felt it. I took the only job I could get: waitressing. My mother loved the baby and was willing to take care of her while I worked, trying to put a little money away because, even though Tim was paying child support, I still couldn't earn enough to make it on my own."

Laura smiled shyly. "You can't imagine what happened next. I had some casual dates but they all turned into nothing worth talking about. As soon as they found out I had a child, they were gone, gone, gone. Then a guy began to come in regularly to the restaurant where I worked and he always sat at one of my tables. After a while he asked me out. This time I made him come home to my house and meet my parents and my baby, Ashley. I wanted to be sure he knew what he would be taking on if he got involved with me. Surprisingly, that didn't scare him away. Gerry was a liquor salesman and he made good money. He took me to the better restaurants, ones where he had the liquor accounts. He taught me how to dress and fix my hair. He insisted I get a manicure every week and he encouraged me to work out so that I wouldn't feel so tired. He bought me designer clothes and helped me to become more sophisticated. Everybody knew Gerry. It was a lot of fun to walk into a restaurant and see him stop and shake someone's hand at almost every table as we were led to ours.

"I was so happy when Gerry asked me to marry him. I was very aware that it isn't easy to find someone who wants you when you already have a child. After we were married, we would pack the baby up on the weekends and go to the stock car races. Gerry was able to get a lot of new accounts at the track. Stock car racing isn't just for grease monkeys and good ol' boys anymore. Investors, stockbrokers, club owners, and restaurateurs are big fans and frequent the tracks. But to tell you the truth, I just couldn't get interested in it. The baby was too little and she would get bored and cranky. Then Gerry would get annoyed with both of us. He wanted to show the baby to the stockbroker-types, the restaurant owners, so they would think he was a responsible family man. He always insisted that I be glad to meet and greet all these different people. I realized too late that the important thing to Gerry was that I look good at all times. He would be so annoyed if I had a cold or hadn't done my hair the way he liked it when we were going out. I guess the thing that confused me was that he had even been interested in me once he learned I had a child. If he had just been looking for some arm candy, there were plenty of pretty girls who would have been glad to go out with him."

Laura sighed. "When I finally got the nerve up to say I wouldn't go to the stock car races anymore and that I didn't think it was a good place for Ashley, Gerry went by himself. But only after he ranted and raved that I didn't understand how important going to the races was to his business. As you can probably guess, it didn't take long for Gerry to replace me with a very pretty girl who was willing to fix her hair the way Gerry wanted, happy to dress the way he told her to, and delighted to eat dinner every night in fancy restaurants and go to the track with him.

"I'm working in a coffee shop in one of the big chain bookstores now, one where they serve all kinds of exotic coffee drinks: cappuccinos, mochas, coffee topped with whipped cream, foreign-sounding herbal teas, and a variety of fancy, expensive cookies. Lots of people come in, sit around for a couple of hours, and read. Waitressing is really the only thing I know how to do. I hope that this is the place where I am going to meet some really nice guy this time."

Laura isn't any better prepared to judge the next man who wanders into her life nor does she have any plans to take control of her life.

There is a gentle softness about Laura, a little-girl fragility, that was sure to attract men to her, men who want to protect and take care of her. However, that very softness also attracted men who wanted to control and mold her.

Notice how, at the end of her story, Laura is still hoping to meet someone, almost accidentally—at the mall, at her workplace—just as she met Tim and Gerry. She is passively waiting for someone to come along and rescue her again. Laura just might find that those rescuers are looking for someone like her to fulfill their own needs, needs that she might not be willing or able to satisfy.

Trevor

Trevor flashed his shy boyish grin as he pushed his Leonardo DiCaprio–style hair back out of his eyes. "Living with me isn't easy," he said, looking up over his glasses. "I'm pretty messy and I guess I drive people nuts because I just don't seem to see all the stuff I leave lying around.

"My first girlfriend, Trude, said that I looked vulnerable, whatever that means, and that was what was so appealing about me." He shrugged. "I think I look pretty strong, able to take care of myself, but that's what she said. I have big plans for my future. I intend to be the next Bill Gates. You know, the president of Microsoft, the richest man in the world. Anyway, I met Trude in the library at school. I had a big pile of computer books spread all over the table and all the nearby chairs, and she had to move some of them out of her way before she could sit down. After a while we got to talking and it turned out that she needed help with one of her papers on statistics. Statistics are a snap for me, but laundry is a really big problem. So we worked out an arrangement—I would help with statistics, she would help with laundry. This worked fine for a couple of months while we got to know each other a little better, and it seemed so logical that since we could both save money, we should move in together. When she first moved into my little off-campus apartment, it seemed ideal. Just roommates, with a trade-off for both of us. But after a few months, it turned into a relationship and then a couple of months later, it turned ugly. She called me, 'a charming narcissist, a slippery chameleon,' and a lot of other names that weren't quite as fancy." Trevor looked really puzzled. "She threw things at me and slammed doors when she left. I still don't really understand what I did wrong."

He hesitated. "There were a couple of others after that. Mary, a very cute blond who was really smart and funny, and then Robin, a tall brunette. I thought Robin was going to be the one because she was really into computers. She was planning to be a high school physics teacher, and we could talk about lots of science things. In fact, she was in a couple of my programming classes. But things went bad with Robin, too. She not only threw stuff, she ended up crashing my hard drive on purpose. Then, when she left, she threw my monitor on the floor where it broke into a zillion pieces." Trevor shrugged his shoulders as if he was getting rid of the memories.

"After a while I realized there was a familiar pattern to these relationships, and I really didn't like what I saw. But I don't know what to do about any of it. These women all seemed to want to take care of me, to 'straighten me out' when I don't want to be straightened out. That sure isn't what I'm looking for. I am who I am, but they just didn't seem to be able to accept that. When I don't 'shape up'—hang up my clothes, remember their birthdays, take out the garbage, act like a husband—then they go out slamming the door, yelling and crying, stomping their feet, and that's the end of that."

Trevor's face was a picture of bewilderment. "I never came on to any of them. They all came on to me and before you knew it, they were at my place, washing out the coffee cups and changing the drapes. Sure, I'd sure like to have someone in my life, but these girls are looking for a permanent relationship before we even know each other. They're studying how they can change me, make me into suitable husband material, almost as soon as I meet them."

Shy and appealing, Trevor's boyish vulnerability was so obvious, it was as if he was issuing an open invitation to young women to smother him with mothering. His very boyishness apparently attracted the type of young women who saw him as pliable clay and wanted to shape his personality, to mold him into the kind of husband they were looking for. But they are exactly the opposite of the women Trevor wants in his life.

Both Laura and Trevor saw that they repeatedly attracted the wrong people in their romantic lives. And although both these young people wanted to do something different, they kept making the same mistakes. They knew they needed to make some changes but didn't seem to have any idea what these changes might be. They had a hard time figuring out how to find a relationship that was permanent, loving, caring, and based on mutual trust.

Laura made a few obvious changes. She changed her hair color and lost a little weight. She bought new clothes and took up roller blading. She even signed up for a class in photography because she heard that men were interested in it. She also went into therapy for a while but decided it was just too expensive for her.

Trevor made some pretty obvious changes, too. He went to Club Med for a week and hated it. He learned a lesson there, that fun in the sun was not the place to find the right woman. Then he got a dog because he heard that women will pet any dog that wags its tail at them, "and someone who likes animals has to have a kind heart." He added offhandedly, "That might be a good way to meet someone interesting." Apparently, all it accomplished was that he now had a big smelly dog, Petey, that slept in his bed, adding to the sloppy disheveled look about him and his apartment, which seemed to charm strangers but actually just helped to mess up his relationships.

You have probably done some of the same things yourself, as most of us have when we realize that we just aren't meeting anyone with the potential for a lasting relationship. Maybe you joined a gym or took a class in something you really weren't interested in. Harmless probably, maybe even beneficial, because you felt better and perhaps learned something new. But often just another waste of time, as far as meeting someone goes. You've gone through Aunt Sarah's list of eligibles and those of all of your friends and everybody under ninety at your church or synagogue.

Your workplace is seriously hurting for anyone who might be a real possibility, although a few think they are hunks or babes, people you might flirt with at the water cooler but nothing more. Perhaps you decided that casual sex, which makes jerks out of men and fools out of women, is a pretty dangerous and nonproductive way to find a permanent relationship. Maybe you quit going to late night clubs, and you feel pretty righteous about that. And just like the rest of us, you gave serious thought to what you can do to meet that reliable, responsible someone who will share your dreams and your life, a person you can trust. Someone who, like you, desires to avoid all the romantic and sexual dilemmas that plague modern relationships. And still, no Mr. or Ms. Right. Just where is that honest, permanent, and monogamous loving relationship you dream of finding?

Both Trevor and Laura began to realize that cosmetic changes weren't much help in their search for true love. While they both knew that some of their behavior was repetitive and somewhat detrimental, they felt stuck in the cycle of habitual patterns they had chosen to deal with their problems. However, they both tried hard to change. They did all the usual things: talked about their current romances over lunch with peers and pals; commiserated with friends whose love lives were going badly, too; read a few books, looking for answers and seeking things they could change about themselves that wouldn't be too painful. They both admitted they read the advice to the lovelorn columns in the daily paper and even *Playboy*. Laura had her horoscope done and Trevor admitted he'd even had his palm read at an art fair. He said he also thought about talking to a priest but felt too embarrassed to ever follow through on that idea.

Neither of them knew much about alternative ways of viewing the universe, other than what they had learned in science or through their exposure to various religions.

Laura had heard about auras and chakras, but she wasn't really sure that she understood what she had heard. She thought they were "some sort of New Age stuff." She admitted that she knew people who had been treated by an acupuncturist for a variety of health problems, and she knew that the acupuncture points were related to the chakras in some way. She trusted her friends who had been treated with acupuncture and whose health had improved, so that made the concept more credible.

Trevor, on the other hand, had never heard of either auras or chakras, although he did know about halos from his Catholic upbringing, having seen them over the heads of saints and religious figures in church and in books. Trevor was all set to resist learning anything about them because he thought they were connected to religion, but when he heard that chakras and auras had something to do with electromagnetic fields, quantum physics, and the transference of energy, he was willing to listen.

The concept of chakras and auras has been around for centuries, long before Sir Isaac Newton described his totally mechanical world. Hundreds of years ago people did not conceive of the universe as a gigantic machine, with everything in it solid and separate from everything else. Before Newtonian science, people accepted a world in which things might be connected and interwoven in mysterious ways. The advent of Newtonian thinking led the world away from the previously accepted understanding of our universe as a connected and interwoven vibrational one, in which various unexplained forces existed.

Not until Einstein's theory of relativity and quantum physics did people once again consider that things appearing solid and separate might not be. Only then did physicists begin to consider that matter of all kinds, including the human body, is vibrating at a rate too rapid for our senses to comprehend and therefore might not be solid or separate at all. Accepting Newton, we accepted the concept that the basic building blocks of this universe were atoms, compact and indestructible, and that these atoms existed in three-dimensional space and their movements followed fixed laws. Newtonian science, while it brought us calculus and an understanding of gravity, created a very limited view of human beings and the world in which we live.

In the mid-twentieth century, the atoms that Newtonian physics defined as indestructible, the most elementary building blocks of the world, were found to be made of even smaller and smaller parts—protons, neutrons, and electrons. Later research would detect even smaller, subatomic particles. Exploration of this subatomic world now reveals that the universe that appears to be composed of solid objects is actually a complex web of vibrating matter exhibiting wavelike properties. We now understand that these interweaving, interfolding fields have properties and possibilities undreamed of in Newtonian science.

Without knowing such science, past cultures and their world-views—Eastern philosophies, shamanism, and mysticism—understood that these boundaries, later to be described by Newton, were actually an illusion. The Hindus and other ancient peoples describe seven major energy centers within the body, which run from the base of the spine up to the top of the head, as well as a number of minor ones. Known as chakras, they are thought to be spinning vortexes of energy, brought in to the body from the universe and generating an electromagnetic field of their own as they whirl. *Chakra* is a Sanskrit word that literally means "wheel of light." These whirling vortexes of energy, these chakras, then produce an aura or energy field that can be felt, sensed, and sometimes seen outside the body. This palpable energy field is called an aura.

The quality and amount of energy located in each chakra reflects how each of us handles the physical, emotional, and spiritual issues in our lives and the aura is the external manifestation of that self, reflecting each person's feelings and emotions. The aura is the energy field of each person, which moves with and surrounds every individual and can extend outward as much as three feet to six feet.

Your aura is an extension of who you are. It tells everyone who comes into contact with you, by generating felt or sensed energy, about your actions, thoughts, emotions, and beliefs. It tells the outside world what you have created in your life and where you are on this life's journey. It contains each person's internal and external experiences; that is, this energy field holds the vibrational patterns of your beliefs and life experiences and communicates those beliefs and experiences to others.

Psychologists tell us that we all make initial judgments about others within the first ten seconds of meeting them. Of course, some of that is based on their physical presence, our past experience with similar-appearing individuals and other factors, but those judgments are often based on no more than just a "feeling," a sense we get about this new person. Our first impression of them is often more lasting and accurate than anything we might later learn about them.

If you've ever said something like, "I don't know what it is. He or she seems pleasant enough; I just get a bad feeling about him or her. That person has bad vibes."

Or, "What energy, she just glowed when she came into the room!," then you have already felt or sensed an aura. We have all met people who have that intangible something known as charisma, people we find fascinating or bewitching, without being able to explain just what it is about them that is so attractive.

When someone's energy field is strong and whole, the individual is strong and whole also. But when the energy of even one of the chakras is drained, weak, or blocked, not only can it affect all the others, it will result in the individual's aura being torn or having holes. Thus, the electromagnetic field that surrounds each individual varies, depending on the energy generated by each chakra, and this will attract or repel the electromagnetic field of other people. Sometimes individuals have energy channels that are so weak or blocked, they continually attract others whose energy fills up those spaces or tears in their own aura. This is seldom beneficial.

There are many reasons why we make the choices we do. Some of it may be genetic, some of it based on past experience and conditioning. However, if for some unknown reason we continually attract the wrong people, individuals who make our lives miserable, then perhaps it is time to consider that we are sending out the wrong signals. Perhaps it is time to learn about chakras, auras, and the energy they generate. It may be that in order to find true love and attract relationships based on mutual trust and respect, we need to repair and heal our auras.

A number of healers work with the energy fields of chakras and auras. Many of them use crystals and/or touch to affect the energy levels of their clients. However, our own thinking, the attitudes we have about the world around us, as well as the strength of our physical body, can be either be a severe energy drain or can be energizing, opening the flow of vigor and well-being into and out of the chakras. As each individual does the healing work of repairing attitudes, altering negative thinking, strengthening the physical body, and grounding it, the chakras will be cleansed and healed, they will open and energy will flow, benefiting the aura, making it whole and beautiful. The result can be happiness, joy, and contentment, because not only will you be doing the right thing for yourself, this raised energy level will be felt and recognized by everyone around you.

Whatever your religious background or philosophical thinking, most of us are familiar with the idea, expressed in a variety of religions and in a number of philosophies, that *we are one*. There can exist a state of being, a level of consciousness, in which this statement becomes true when your aura is healthy and whole. This is a magnificent feeling of unity, of merging your soul or your energy with another person's, when you are so much in love that you feel that your very soul has joined with that of another; or in a church or religious community, the sense of belonging can be sublime, when you feel connected to everyone in the group who is working toward a common goal. This state of being at one with something or someone has been experienced as joyful and spiritual by saints and religious figures throughout recorded history. Unblocking the chakras and energizing your aura will lead to finding this mystical path for locating your companion and friend for life, your true soul mate for the future.

After both Laura and Trevor were assured that healing their auras would never be physically painful, could only be beneficial, and would merely require them to devote some time to tasks and exercises, they were both eager to begin.

When it was suggested to Trevor that his fourth chakra, which determined his ability to see himself, was probably blocked, Trevor just shrugged his shoulders. He agreed that he was open to making some changes, actually already knew that he needed to change, but he asked, "How will I know when I've opened or strengthened it, or whatever it is I will be doing to my chakras and my aura? I already understand that most people can't see them." He laughed as he said this because he thought the whole concept very "New Age." He could, however, understand that while it didn't matter whether or not he ever saw an aura, as his energy field changed, its electromagnetic effect on others around him would automatically alter. Good-natured, Trevor agreed he would give it a try.

As Trevor began to work through the tasks and exercises to strengthen his energy field and heal his aura, he found that people reacted to him in a more positive way. During his first task of examining his role model, he realized for the first time that he really didn't know very much about Bill Gates as a person. Trevor already felt very strongly about what he wanted to do with his life, but by putting all his energy and emphasis on computers and math he had neglected the humane part of himself. He had unconsciously recognized some of that need when he got the dog. Yet he had actually added to his message that he needed mothering when he presented women with two creatures who needed care instead of one—himself and his undisciplined dog, Petey. As he brought these two areas of his life, work and humanity, more into balance, he found that women no longer needed to "fill in" the part of his aura that projected his need for someone to take care of him. They no longer had such a desire to minister to his neediness for nurturing, a part of himself that he had so long ignored.

Laura had a number of chakras that were weak and without energy. She readily accepted that as a result, her aura had some large holes in it, attracting the energy of strong, willful men who wanted to mold her into someone who reflected well on them, men she didn't have the strength to resist. It was consistent with Laura's softness that she never questioned what she was being asked to do. When she was asked to dress up, fix her hair a certain way, and act charming to buddies and pals of Tim and Gerry, she simply became just another one of the accessories to their lives. Laura was anxious to do something new, and she thought the idea of changing her energy fields and affecting how others sensed her sounded like fun.

After about a month, Laura expressed her amazement, "I just can't believe it. I'm finding that an entirely different kind of man is talking to me now, men are treating me with a respect and courtesy I have never experienced before!" As Laura's chakra energy increased and her aura became whole, her self-esteem improved dramatically. The result was that Laura began presenting herself in an entirely different manner. She became more in control of herself; she didn't allow herself to waste time just looking for the next rescuer. She decided to go back to school and get her high school diploma. She expressed an interest in a field she had never considered before—becoming a dental hygienist.

Both Laura and Trevor report that the tasks and exercises have made the concept of chakras and auras come alive for them. "When I did some of the tasks, I found myself considering that I was not just performing an exercise, I was altering an invisible electromagnetic field, and I found that very stimulating. In fact, it made me do some of the exercises I might have just skipped over otherwise," reported Trevor.

Laura agreed, "I really got into the exercises, especially simple things, like keeping the food diary for a week. Thinking about changing something that is going on inside of me rather than just giving up a few treats made it a whole lot easier to do".

Trevor and Laura had a lot of fun exploring this new world of energy fields. When asked if they found their lives improved, they both answered with a resounding "Yes!"

2 The Human Energy Field: Is This Why You Send Strangers the Wrong Message?

Love, the quest; marriage, the conquest;
divorce, the inquest.

—Helen Rowland
American writer 1875–1950

A large body of research exists concerning the study of human energy. Much of the resulting data has provided amazing information that resulted in discoveries that proved helpful to mankind. Frequently, scientific investigations are pursued only when it is shown that these discoveries will eventually produce some benefit or prove financially profitable.

Research has scientifically shown the electromagnetic and chemical behavior of the human body and mind. It has long been known that each organ in the body generates a characteristic electrical field that can be detected on the skin's surface. The laws of physics state that any electrical current is accompanied by a corresponding magnetic field in the surrounding space, but since the magnetic fields of life were too tiny to detect, until recently biologists assumed that they had no real significance.

The electrocardiograph, or EKG, and the encephalograph, or EEG, are accepted as valid scientific documentation of the ability of sophisticated machinery to register the electrical activity of both the human heart and the human brain. These traditional electrical recordings are now being complemented by biomagnetic recordings, magnetocardiograms, and magnetoencephalograms. Another diagnostic tool that produces images of any part of the body is Magnetic Resonance Imaging, or MRI. These images are created because the body is filled with small biological magnets that constantly emit electromagnetic transmissions that can be "heard." Physicians and physical therapists in the United States currently use electric current to speed up the healing of a variety of wounds, including broken and fractured bones, because it has been shown that by delivering exogenous electrical signals into wound tissue, it is possible to mimic the electrical charges of the body's natural bioelectrical system and stimulate the formation of growth factor receptors

In a rather new field of quantum medicine (also known as bioelectricity), the healing power of magnetism is being studied and developed. Scientists at three universities in China are studying a new microchip technology because they believe the human body is a complex electromagnetic/chemical system living in a world of electromagnetic energy fields. Microchips that emit a low-intensity electrical field are placed at acupuncture points and have been shown to aid in lowering blood pressure, relieving the discomfort of certain joint conditions, speeding the repair of bone fractures, calming the nerves of those suffering from anxiety conditions, and relieving a variety of symptoms, from headaches to heart palpitations. In Europe pure magnetic fields are being studied as a means of shrinking tumors and in the treatment of rheumatoid and degenerative arthritis. Currently, a number of well-known athletes promote the use magnets in bracelets and belts for the relief of pain.

Modern practitioners of QiGong accept that the inner energy known as qi is, in fact, bioelectricity and, as a QiGong practitioner moves his body through the static magnetic fields that exist around him, this movement generates tiny electrical currents in the body in the same manner as acupuncture. In public demonstrations of the power of these electric currents and what can be done by someone trained to control and focus this inner energy, very tiny female QiGong masters provide amazing demonstrations of their abilities, by moving other, much larger, individuals backward without ever physically touching them, using only the power of their focused and concentrated inner energy.

"Although it might look like some kind of magic, it is actually the ability to harness and concentrate the energy of the universe," said QiGong master Dennis Chung. "Every student of QiGong develops physical, mental, and spiritual awareness and these elements transcend to a higher level, to a life lived very differently. Through this energy, self-awareness and self-respect become a goal, and ultimately QiGong becomes a way of life."

In his book *Cross Currents* Dr. Robert Becker writes that "All living things are surrounded by a magnetic field that extends out into space from our bodies. The implications of this are enormous."

Twentieth-century Russian researchers S. D. and V. I. Kirlian developed a process using ultraviolet light to photograph a faint, glowing band of light surrounding the outline of an object. This process, first used to document the energy of living plants, is known as Kirlian photography. It is thought to be produced by the electronic and ionic interactions caused by the electrical field that surrounds not only plants, but all living things. Science has not developed a practical use for Kirlian photography at the present time, although it is obvious that they are photographing, and making visible for anyone who wishes see it, the energy field known as the aura. While it seems that we can photograph this aura, the difficulty, at the present time, is interpreting that photographic image.

The Mysterious Universe

There was a time when anything that was not understood had a mystical explanation. If a physical phenomenon didn't have a readily comprehensible reason for its occurrence, then it could be attributed to the working of the gods, who were superhuman with magical powers. People believed that the sound of thunder was produced by Thor's chariot as he roared across the sky, that fire-breathing dragons existed, and that the world was flat. No one doubted that powerful demons roamed the world, that mermaids lured sailors to their death, and that creatures such as the gorgon Medusa had living snakes for hair.

Ptolemy, the Roman astronomer and mathematician, who was believed to have lived around A.D. 100, dominated scientific thought with his theories until the sixteenth century. In his most famous work, the *Almagest,* he proposed a geometric theory to account for the apparent motions and positions of the planets, sun, and moon against a background of unmoving stars. He readily accepted the prevailing theory of the world as the people of his time knew it. It was believed then that the earth was the unmoving center of the universe and that the planets and stars moved continuously in perfectly circular orbits around it. Ptolemy elaborated on the theory by proposing that the planets, sun, and moon moved in small circles around much larger circles, in which the earth was centered. In his work *Geography* he employed a system of longitude and latitude that influenced map makers and other mathematicians for hundreds of years, although it was not reliable.

It was not until the Polish astronomer Copernicus, in the sixteenth century, argued that the sun was the center of the universe and that the earth, spinning on its axis and wobbling like a top, revolved around the sun daily, that anyone began to think differently about the universe and how it worked. Even then, it was more than another hundred years before English mathematician Sir Isaac Newton invented calculus, formulated the science of dynamics, and "discovered" gravity, and then more than another hundred years before the world's view of cosmology began to change.

The Mechanical Universe

In the seventeenth century Newton established the modern science of dynamics by formulating his three laws of motion. When he applied these laws to the laws of orbital motion formulated by the German astronomer Johannes Kepler, he derived the law of universal gravitation. Although people at that time knew by simple observation that when apples ripened on trees, they fell to the ground, and when anything, such as an arrow, was launched upward into the sky it would fall back down to earth, no one could really explain why.

Newton, the mathematician and physicist, gave the world a basic law that explained how all objects in space and on earth were affected by a single force—gravity. Newton's gravitational theory marked a turning point in science. Applying Newton's laws of motion to everything in the universe, philosophers began to view the universe and all in it as a huge complex of machines. One of the laws of motion stated that nothing would move without another thing exerting pressure or some type of force upon it. As a result, everything was seen as a solid object with pistons, pumps, gears, wheels, cogs, and pulleys. Everything became mechanical, including the human body, which was viewed as having fixed parts, as being predictable, and as operating within a closed system. The human body was depicted as no more than another type of mechanism, with a heart that pumped blood through intricate plumbing.

Everything, whether animate or inanimate, whether large or small, was seen as simply another solid object with movable parts within this universe. There was nothing in the world that wasn't solid, including buildings, trees, people, and animals. When you looked at something as small as a frog's toenail or as large as a mountain, they were all seen as separate solid objects. As a result of Newton's theories, we were visited with the concept of an entire universe, including the planets above the earth, the rocks, and the oceans of the earth, which were all subject to these basic laws. Newton's world was a gigantic machine made up of smaller machines.

As his theories were developed by others, smaller and smaller particles were discovered and, although they followed Newton's laws of motion and gravity, they still appeared to be solid and separate. Atoms, with a nucleus or center of protons, with neurons and electrons revolving around that center, followed the same rules as the planets above us, orbiting around the sun.

The Everyday Universe

Hundreds of years later, most of us still view the world in Newtonian terms because we experience it mostly through our senses of sight and hearing, in three-dimensional space and linear time. We are not surprised to see the sun rise every morning and travel across the sky and even an elementary school student can grasp the concept that a car moves forward because of the traction of its tires against the asphalt. We can all look at a couch or a chair and know absolutely that, although the couch and the chair are made up of atoms of different materials, they are solid and both will support us if we choose to sit down on them.

We've all heard of nuclear power plants, we've seen spectacular TV coverage as NASA blasts rockets off into space, as tall buildings are imploded and fall into themselves in a matter of minutes, and we have casually joined hundreds of other people in boarding jet planes that will take us thousands of miles in just a few hours, without fearing that they will fall out of the sky, even though they weigh hundreds of tons. We've learned a lot of new words such as cyberspace, Internet, Kevlar, and slamming. A few of us know a little something about how all of these things work, some know a little more about one or the other, but the majority of us accept that electricity from nuclear power, rockets launching, buildings imploding, jet planes flying overhead, the Internet, and whatever happens in cyberspace are all "things" that are made up of atoms of some kind. Although we all see that they work, and can be excited and interested in the event, most of us have very little understanding of how.

The New Millennium Universe

By the 1960s physicist John Bell postulated that subatomic particles are connected to each other in ways that go beyond time and space. He arrived at his conclusion, known as Bell's theorem, not long after the concepts of Einstein and Planck were validated by many others.

Most of us have heard of Einstein's Theory of Relativity, which states that space is not three dimensional and time is not separate. Every high school kid, including me, probably suffered through some science class where an attempt was made to explain this theory. While many teachers attempt to make science "fun," only students who are really interested in it get more than a vague understanding of the theory, plus the idea that this concept is somehow important. Einstein suggested a four-dimensional universe, which is now known as the space-time continuum. In Einstein's thinking, energy and mass are interchangeable. Things that we have thought of as solid are not; everything that appears solid is simply some form of energy moving at a differing vibrational rate.

Not as well known as Einstein, twentieth-century physicist and Nobel laureate Max Planck is the originator of what is known as quantum physics. Planck suggests that we live in a multi-tracked universe and on each track of this varied universe, the rules for time, space, and matter are quite different from those on every other track. In Planck's universe, the submicroscopic world of quantum particles, an electron can move from one orbit around the nucleus of an atom to another orbit without ever crossing the space between the orbits. This happens without movement, without measurable time for the crossing, and without the electron becoming a different kind of matter. In Planck's universe, none of these particles, these atoms with their electrons, protons, and neutrons are solid, but rather they are collections of energy.

Planck's theories became the basis for an entirely new field of physics known as quantum mechanics. Space is not three dimensional, time is not a separate entity, space and time are connected in a four-dimensional or a multidimensional space-time continuum. The solid mechanistic world of Newton, where everything is separate, has now given way to a universe in which energy and mass are interchangeable and things that appear to be solid are simply forms of energy vibrating at different rates. Quantum physics of today describes the human being as composed of energy fields within energy fields, and supports the concept that we are made up mostly of vibrating waves and particles.

The Vibrational Universe

Experimental metaphysics is a name given to some of the more advanced theories of quantum and particle physicists who believe that all living matter is enveloped in electromagnetic fields. In these theories, light is a particle and also a wave: not a real physical wave such as one of sound or water, but a probability wave representing the probability of *interconnections*.

Nobel prize winner physicist David Bohm has stated that ours is "a universe of implicate unfolded and enfolded order." By this statement Bohm means that everything in the universe is immediately connected to everything else and interdependent. Thus, our experimental metaphysical universe is never solid, but is made up of a web of interacting and interweaving energy force fields, vibrating probability waves of light, enveloped in electromagnetic fields. It is a universe where the rules of time and space are very different from those Newton understood. In such a universe, each person is an inseparable part of the whole and, as such, can connect immediately and completely to all of its power and energy.

Biofeedback

Biofeedback equipment, electronic monitoring of the muscle tension created by thoughts and emotions in a body, is available in many pain and stress management clinics today. It is a recognized legitimate tool for teaching people about what is going on in their bodies, how to control it, and how to alter or reduce it. Hooked up to the equipment, a client learns to respond to a light or a sound and then to be in control of their own reactions. By consciously learning to control what were previously thought to be involuntary homeostatic systems in the body, biofeedback has proved that the body/mind complex is an intricate web of electromagnetic waves that change and can be changed by our becoming aware of them.

Biofeedback is proof, by what is considered "legitimate" science, that the electromagnetic systems in the body do exist and can be altered by conscious thought.

The Holographic Universe

Lasers are no longer a mysterious beam of light or the death ray of science fiction. They are in use everywhere. It is now even possible to buy a laser pointer at a convenience store. They are used in a wide variety of surgeries, gun sights, video discs, and fiber optic telecommunications, just to name a few of their applications. They are a very special type of light, known as coherent light, and this light is used to create a kind of picture known as a hologram. Coherent light waves are not scattered but are orderly, following along behind each other in a neat and tidy fashion.

Possibly, you've seen the pictures for sale in the mall that not only appear three dimensional but change as you walk past them. These holograms demonstrate something unique and basic to our understanding of auras—every piece can contain the essence of the whole. Looking at a hologram, we now have before us a visible and unique model for understanding the energetic structure of the universe.

A hologram is made by sending a single laser beam through an optical device that is called a beam splitter. This splitter creates two laser beams out of the single originating laser. One of these, designated the "reference beam," passes through a diffusing lens that causes it to become spread out into a flashlight-like beacon, rather than a very focused pencil-thin ray of light. This reference beam is then guided by mirrors to fall upon an unexposed photographic plate. The second beam, now called the "working beam," passes through a second diffusing lens and is used to illuminate whatever object is being photographed, where it bounces off the object and then falls upon the photographic plate. When the pure reference beam meets with the reflected light of the working beam, they mix and interact and an interference pattern comes into existence. This interference pattern, created by the coherent light of the laser and captured on film, produces a phenomena known as a hologram. The result is a truly three-dimensional image.

When looking at certain holograms, we can walk all around the image and see it as it would look from above, below, and behind. If you cut away a portion of one of these holograms and hold it up to laser light, you will see an entire, intact three-dimensional image of the thing photographed. For example, if you cut out a section of a picture of an orange, when you hold it up to the laser light you will see a picture of the entire orange. Although difficult to comprehend, the hologram is an energy interference pattern and within this pattern, every piece contains the whole. If you choose to cut one of these holograms into tiny pieces, and then view each tiny piece through a laser light, you will see complete but smaller versions of the original hologram.

The concept that "every piece contains the whole" can be seen in the recent experiment at the Roslin Institute in Edinburgh, where scientists created a sheep named Dolly using a single cell from a six-year-old animal to obtain the DNA blueprint to make an entire sheep. We now call this cloning, a concept that until very recently seemed to be just something from science fiction.

What does this mean to the concept of auras? It gives us a new way of looking at the universe and comprehending energy fields within and around the human body. The aura, the energy field that surrounds each human, is an example of "every piece contains the whole" because it embodies all the information about each individual's emotional, physical, and spiritual condition.

The Chakra and Aura Universe

For those who might consider the idea of chakras and auras nothing more than New Age gobbledygook, remember that new ideas always seem strange until someone demonstrates their existence and then their usefulness.

Centuries ago the Chinese recognized that when an iron object was stroked with the mineral lodestone, it attracted another piece of iron, but this information was useless until about 1200 when a crude magnetic compass was used by sailors for navigation. It was not until 1600 that English physician Gilbert realized that the earth behaves like a giant magnet, and he published the very first study of electrical and magnetic phenomena.

In the 1700s Benjamin Franklin flew his kite in a thunderstorm and demonstrated that atmospheric electricity causes lightning. In the next century Samuel B. Morse showed that you can transmit messages by electrical impulses, and the telegraph was born. The spectacular inventions of Thomas Edison, such as the electric light bulb, sound recording, and motion pictures, soon followed. British physicist and chemist Michael Faraday, pioneer of the electric dynamo, found that fields of force were able to interact with each other and demonstrated that electromagnetic fields travel through space in the forms of waves.

In the 1920s Sir Edward Appleton used radio echoes to determine the height of the atmosphere, and radar was invented.

In a very short period in history, electricity, magnetism, radio, motion pictures, television, radar, and sonar, to name a few, were discoveries that resulted from the recognition that fields of force were always "out there" and that they could be harnessed and utilized in ways that were useful to mankind.

Many cultures have described the energy fields of the human body. Almost every culture has recognized that some kind of an elemental "life force" exists. Hippocrates knew it as *vis medicatrix naturae,* the Chinese call it *chi* or *qi,* the yogis of India named it *prana.* The Japanese speak of *ki,* the Hawaiians of *mana,* and the Tibetans of *tumo.* The Chinese structure their universe out of ever-changing energies, and the balance and harmony of these energies is called *tao.* Tao contains the totality of all the *qi* energy. It exists in a constant state of movement and change, out of which all things evolve. Out of the oneness of Tao there evolves two, yang (masculine) and yin (feminine). This is illustrated by two perfect circles evolving and revolving, the tails of each indicating moment, or an eternal revolution. If you think for a moment, you will remember seeing that symbol, which is used to describe this energy, the dark energy of yin and the bright energy of yang, in many places in modern culture such as T-shirts, books, and CD covers. According to Chinese lore, the body has twelve canals related to vital organs, and they circulate the two principles of yang and yin. By puncturing the canals with small needles, bad secretions or obstructions are permitted to escape and this restores the body's equilibrium.

Various cultures have described the routes of this energy through the human body by a variety of names. One of the more familiar to Western minds is the Sanskrit term, the *chakras.*

If we think about it, many words and symbols that have entered the general language describe this ever-changing energy, so it should not be difficult for us to accept such a concept. However, no matter what different cultures have called this energy or how they describe it, almost every culture has felt that such energy fields do exist and can be manipulated and altered through acupuncture, acupressure, breathing, meditation, exercise, or a variety of other techniques. Often these cultures and their ancient schools of healing have described such higher systems as part of a human multidimensional anatomy. Although these words or others that describe this energy are in our lexicon, Western science has chosen to ignore such descriptions of ethereal components of physiology because their existence could not be documented by anatomical dissection. An acupuncture point, a meridian, a chakra, or an aura have not been seen under a microscope, and only now, as Western technology has evolved, are we beginning to achieve confirmation that such subtle-energy systems actually do exist and as such, they can influence a human's smallest of cells.

Other writers, such as Rosalyn Bruyere in *Wheels of Light,* describe these energy fields in Native American culture, in the ancient traditions of the Egyptians and Greeks, and in the philosophies of the Hindus and other peoples of the East; and NASA scientist Barbara Ann Brennan, in *Hands of Light,* recounts her fifteen years of professional experience with the human energy field.

Dr. Candace Pert, a neurobiologist, said that neuropeptides—the chemicals triggered by emotions—are thoughts converted into matter. Appearing with Bill Moyers on public television's *Healing and the Mind,* Dr. Pert said, "Clearly, there is another form of energy that we have not yet understood. For example, there is a form of energy that appears to leave the body when the body dies. There are many phenomena that we cannot explain without going into the concept of energy."

Dr. Richard Gerber, a physician who practices internal medicine in Michigan, believes that humans are made up of light waves that he calls "frozen light." Following the theories of such physicists as Planck and Bohm, Gerber says that the human only appears to be solid. He writes in his book *Vibrational Medicine* that "each human being is an organized interweaving of many bodies of differing vibrational frequencies and through . . . the chakras and our higher frequency bodies we are able to assimilate energy and information from the highest levels of being." He believes that the human being is a series of interacting multidimensional subtle-energy systems, and if these energy systems become imbalanced, it may result in pathological symptoms that are manifest on not only the physical, but on the emotional, mental, and spiritual planes. "When the human being is weakened or is out of balance, this energy will oscillate at a different or less-harmonic frequency. Due to the limited nature of the physical brain . . . we become locked into the perspective of a seemingly fixed space/time frame. Thus, the multidimensional universe is beyond our undeveloped insight."

If scientists such as Einstein, Planck, Bell, and Bohm have postulated a universe that is a vast interweaving and interconnected collection of different kinds of energy fields, all moving, flowing, interacting, pulsating, each at its proper rate but in harmony with all the others, and have demonstrated through the science of quantum physics and quantum mechanics that such energy fields exist, then it is quite possible that in the future it will be proved that these same energy fields can enter and leave our bodies through the energy centers known as chakras, and can be manifest outside our bodies in the form of vibrational energy known as auras.

Find the Light

A universe of interweaving and intersecting universe of energy fields—magnetic and electric, a giant web of energy, pulsating and flowing, is out there, waiting to connect with you and through you. Your aura is made up of electromagnetic waves and is a man-ifestation of your true self. It extends outward from your body at least three to six feet and while it can be seen by a few, it can *always* be felt or sensed by others. *This energy attracts and repels others.* It doesn't lie, but if you don't like what it tells the world about you, you can change and then—*you can alter it!*

At the present time more and more people are leaving tradi-tional medicine and searching in the field of alternative medicine for ways to treat their physical and emotional ills. Interest in herbal remedies, exotic treatments with the aid of Native American med-icine men, Eastern gurus, acupuncturists, and others, as well as a myriad of other nontraditional therapies, have gained the attention of millions. Ancient wisdoms have long taught that there are meth-ods to alter the energy fields we call chakras and auras, and these include breathing techniques, meditation, prayer, the laying on of hands, diet, exercise, and many other alterations to lifestyle.

A number of health practitioners have entered the field, includ-ing nurses, chiropractors, psychotherapists, and physicians, and they all report instances of clients who have cried, relived life experi-ences, or experienced visions during their treatment. In some in-stances, those being treated for a physical ailment with one of these nontraditional techniques found that the thoughts that arose during treatment were so painful that the experience left them exhausted and they chose not to continue or return, not understanding that they connected with a way to completely alter their lives by un-blocking or re-energizing their chakras and their auras.

The American Holistic Nurses Association teaches and certifies nurses to use their hands above a patient's body in a method known as Healing Touch, which manipulates energy fields. This practice emphasizes the inner development of the practitioner; it is a prerequisite that she intend the highest good toward the patient. In a recent newsletter they wrote, "Spirituality and science have been kept separate since the scientific era, but more and more we are seeing the holism of all creation, the connectedness of every-one and everything, and the re-emergence of science and spiritual-ity as different perspectives of the same thing."

This concept of the inner development of the practitioner is very important to think about regarding the manipulation of your energy fields by another. Those who have studied the shamans and gurus of other cultures observed that they often spent years in preparation, performing ritual cleansings of their own psyche, along with learning the necessary skills of their art and profession. Any practitioner, particularly in our Western culture, whether they are chiropractors, acupuncturists, psychotherapists, aromatherapists, or others, may have documented phenomenal results and may be well-intentioned, but may not have the inner spiritual development to "do no harm." If you wish assistance, you should have no difficulty finding a therapist schooled in any number of eclectic energy techniques who will work with you.

But before you allow someone to attempt to alter your energy fields, you should have a clear understanding of their intent and purpose. Better yet, alter your aura yourself.

It is entirely possible to work with your own energy fields. Since one of the laws of physics states that "Energy can neither be created nor destroyed, it can only be transformed," then energy in the form of your thoughts and your emotions can be used to expand or limit your chakras—*you can transform yourself.*

It may ultimately be more rewarding and satisfying, in a gratifying journey of self-discovery and renewal, to explore and modify, expand and energize your own chakras and your own aura.

It is my belief that each of us really knows what we need and how to find it. Perform the tasks and exercises, bring unconscious material up to your own consciousness at your own pace, examine it, study it, meditate on it quietly, and as you do so, you will then effortlessly heal and alter your own aura. It will happen and when it does, you will see the changes you need and wish for occurring in your life.

3 The Mysterious Chakras Explained: They Aren't So Mysterious After All

> What is necessary to change a person
> is to change his awareness of himself.
>
> —Abraham H. Maslow

People of ancient cultures, including the Egyptians, the Chinese, the East Indians, and Native Americans, in their art, writings, and teachings, have all described wheels of energy within the human body. Although they may have called them names other than *chakras,* or described them differently, they all taught that there were flows of energy from the universe that course through each and every living thing, vitalizing it, and then flowing outward again, into the universe.

An Ocean of Energy

If you are willing to accept such a concept—one that quantum physics now says is reality—that we are all swimming in an ocean of energy; that the entire universe is one inseparable whole, a vast web of interweaving energy; that each of us is engulfed in waves of energy that cross each other and intermingle; that these waves of energy emit vibrations that can be transmitted across all living tissue, in and out of all systems, then the concept of chakras, spinning disks of celestial energy, stimulating and being stimulated by each person's physical, emotion, spiritual, and mental being, and projecting an invisible manifestation of that person to the world in very individual waves of energy—then the idea of these disks, these *chakras,* will be neither mysterious nor difficult to understand.

Chakras

The word *chakra* means "wheel" in Sanskrit, and because of the interest in Eastern religions in the 1960s this word quickly entered into the lexicon of the West. It is the most recognized word used to describe this energy flow from the universe. In the Hindu cosmology chakras are described as small, dully colored disks, approximately the size of a silver dollar, located in the astral body. They whirl with energy drawn from and exchanged with the universe. The astral body is the equivalent of a person's soul; it is immaterial, spiritistic, and does not exist in any physical sense, but that does not mean it is any less real.

Ancient traditions say that as a person matures, these dull disks, the chakras, open like brightly colored flowers. In some beautifully illustrated old literature they are often depicted as glorious lotus blossoms. Because the lotus is sacred in India, growing up from mud, they are symbolic of a long path of physical and spiritual development. They are used to illustrate the process of each individual evolving from a simple, mindless child into a fully blooming, mature, and aware person. Each lotus flower, or chakra, has a number of petals that relate to that particular chakra and each of these petals is described as smaller whirlpools of spinning energy that rotate at extremely high rates.

The individual chakras are described by the ancient literature as energy centers that are connected to each other through an energy channel that runs behind and parallel with the spine. They appear, to those who have studied them, as cone-shaped spinning wheels that are wide at the opening on the outside of the body (about the size of a fist) and narrow where they connect to the internal column or core of energy alongside the spinal column. They all extend out from the front and back of the body, with the exception of the crown chakra, which extends out of the top of the head, and the root chakra, which extends out of the base of the spine. Each chakra is described as corresponding to a particular part of the physical body simply so that it can be visualized and more easily understood.

The Physical

Modern medicine has drawn a relationship between the chakras and the glands of the endocrine system that produce the hormones, which influence bodily functions. These hormones are influenced by the individual's state of physical health as well as his or her thoughts. A simple example of how thoughts alter the endocrine system, and thus the chakras, might be to visualize yourself sitting at home thinking about something or someone exciting, or watching an action adventure or horror film on TV. Your heart will beat faster, your blood pressure will rise, your rate of breathing will increase, and the muscles throughout your body will tense although you have not moved from your chair and are not actually participating in anything exciting or adventurous. When these physiological changes happen, although you are completely unaware of it, you can be sure that the energy flow in and out of your chakras has also been altered.

The Spiritual

Cabalistic mysticism compares experiencing the energy of the chakras to understanding the nature of the divine world and its hidden connections with the world of creation. Other philosophies use the chakras to gauge each person's general state of being and preparedness to undertake the tasks of life.

Today and Yesterday

Modern and ancient theories of the chakras agree that understanding the chakra system and how these energy centers work can be a tool for personal growth in all areas of a person's life.

A chakra can become damaged or cracked, or it can tilt out of alignment with the connecting energy channel. Most of today's experts believe that anything that upsets an individual's normal functioning can potentially disturb the functioning of the chakras and their energy channels. It is important to realize that a memory—any memory—both positive and negative, can become lodged in a chakra and distort or obstruct the flow of energy to or from that chakra. Physical as well as psychological problems can result from these blockages, and repetition of the same behaviors and the same thoughts can keep a chakra blocked for years, preventing someone from moving on in their emotional and spiritual development, keeping them in the same kind of negative relationships, and causing them to repeat harmful thoughts and behaviors over and over again.

From Chakras to Auras

The chakras have a variety of purposes. They are the location of seven basic energy centers within what is known as the *subtle body,* a body that is superimposed upon your physical body. Their functions is to transmit energy both from and to the universe, to vitalize the aura, and to help each individual develop into a mature human being who participates in the workings of the universe. Each individual's belief system, emotions at the moment, and the thoughts and memories that have created them are transmitted by this energy to the outside world.

Chakras are your power centers; they energize every part of your being, and through them you create a personal, palpable energy field that radiates outward from your body in the form of an aura, that truly represents the unique you to the world around you. This chakra energy, which is projected outward by an aura, is what others sense about you. The energy you project cannot be hidden or disguised from the world but, if your own chakras are out of kilter, you may have difficulty interpreting the manifested energy of others and that may prevent you from recognizing negative people and potentially bad relationships.

Every living thing on the planet has an aura, created by the energy of the chakras. This flow of energy is unconscious and you interpret it by hearing, seeing, tasting, feeling, and intuiting it. If you have an unpleasant experience, it is very normal to react to it by blocking out that emotional response to avoid feeling angry, sad, or overwhelmed. Such emotional blocking halts the natural flow of energy. However, if you repeatedly misinterpret what you hear, see, taste, and feel and, as a result, alter or block this energy flow, your aura will be distorted and dull.

Blocking Your Energy Flow

Continually blocking your chakra energy flow can result in all sorts of physical, emotional, and ethical problems. If some chakras are closed, tilted, cracked, or blocked, then you not only do not get the needed energy to and from the universe, you do not get the information you need about the world around you and you do not transmit the proper message about yourself to others. The quality and quantity of energy that is present in our lives is dependent upon how open or closed a particular chakra is at a particular time. If a chakra is "stuck," then it will need healing to remove what is creating the problem. When your chakras are out of synch, you may repeatedly enter into bad relationships, make poor judgments about all sorts of situations, become confused about what you should do with your life, and make errors in decisions about your future.

As we all know, judgment errors about people, careers, and finances can easily result in many regrets. Misinterpreting chakra energy can cause you to think you are in love with the wrong person. Regretfully, many will make this same error more than once. After a series of disappointments, you may think you will never find anyone who is right for you and, until you alter the energy flow of blocked or tilted chakras, you may not find your Mr. or Ms. Right. For example:

If you have a closed third chakra (personal power) or fifth chakra (communication skills), you may fear to speak in public. A problem with the second chakra (sexuality), or fourth chakra (ability to love), may cause an individual to have many sexual partners while never being able to truly love any of them.

Functioning Chakras

When the chakras are open and functioning correctly, they spin clockwise to bring in the needed energy from the universe, which provides you with information about the world around you. Properly functioning chakras also send energy from each individual out into the universe and thus provides others with information about your functioning in the world through the electromagnetic display of that information through your aura.

As you work through the exercises and the tasks, you may not know just which chakra needs to be unblocked or repaired, but that is unimportant because eventually, as you follow along with each chapter, exploring your thoughts and beliefs, the chakras that need to be altered will respond, become healthier, and as a result your entire energy channel will become clear and activated. As you experience a deeper understanding of your own state of consciousness and begin to change your thinking and behavior, your aura will glow with the right kind of energy. As a result, the world will experience you as a changed person, who has brought unconscious thoughts into consciousness, changed them, and thus automatically energized your aura.

The Major Chakras

The location of the seven major chakras corresponds to the major nerve plexuses of the physical body and they all, individually and separately, exchange energy with the universe. The major chakras are often illustrated as being located on the front of the body but in actuality since they are each a locus of energy, there is a similar identifiable site on the back. When thinking about the chakras, you can actually visualize them from any viewpoint.

A number of philosophies and books describe the functioning of the chakras, some of it in language that focuses on the physical,

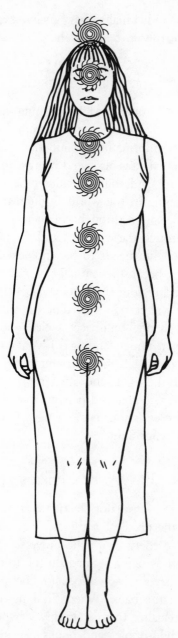

THE MAJOR CHAKRAS

some on the spiritual, and some on the psychological. In addition to their overall function as energy transmitters, four of the chakras have an aspect that is associated with one of the elements, which were once thought to be fundamental constituents of the universe, as well as having a particular function in your life. While these philosophies may use different language to describe this association, they are often described as follows:

Root Chakra—1

Location: At the base of the spine
Element: Earth
Function: Grounding, survival, physical activities of the body, beginnings, unity

Sacral Chakra—2

Location: At the pubic area, the reproductive organs
Element: Water
Function: Pleasure, desire, sexuality, procreation, emotions, duality

Solar Plexus Chakra—3

Location: At the abdomen, the navel
Element: Fire
Function: Personal power, energy, will, transformation, self-interest

Heart Chakra—4

Location: At the heart
Element: Air
Function: Love, humanity, relationships, affinity, healing

Throat Chakra—5

Location: At the middle of the throat

Function: Communication, truth, creativity, responsibility,
           nourishment

Third Eye Chakra—6

Location: Between the eyebrows
Function: Visualization, intuition, imagination, humanity,
           wisdom, compassion

Crown Chakra—7

Location: Top of the head
Function: Spirituality, enlightenment, knowledge, thought,
           understanding, meditation

The chakras are also associated with certain colors and gem-
stones or minerals. People who have worked with the chakras for
a long time believe that being aware of the color and the mineral
associated with that chakra and using both the color and the mineral in meditation can often have beneficial effects.

Minerals

Mineralogists classify crystals based on the geometric patterns of
their formations. Those who believe that minerals are related to
particular chakras base that on the concept that there is a relationship between the vibratory energy of each mineral and a corresponding chakra.

Chakra	Crystal Classification	Typical Mineral
Crown	Triclinic	Turquoise
Third Eye	Monoclinic	Jade
Throat	Orthorhombic	Topaz
Heart	Tetragonal	Copper
Solar Plexus	Hexagonal	Emerald
Sacral	Cubic	Diamond
Root	Trigonal	Amethyst

Centuries before modern science discovered wavelengths and color spectrums, people associated specific colors with the chakras, corresponding to the seven colors of the rainbow. Or, from the lowest wavelength frequency to the highest, as follows: red—root, orange—sacral, yellow—solar plexus, green—heart, blue—throat, indigo—third eye, and violet—crown.

However, various Hindu texts often describe them as: yellow—root, white—sacral, red—solar plexus, smoky—heart, blue—throat, gold—third eye, and finally, for the crown chakra, a "color" of luster beyond color.

Modern systems of chakra color associations often state that all colors are present in each and every chakra, flowing and streaming in and out as they form patterns and reflect the individual's life at that moment. However, most of these modern systems believe that if the individual is physically, emotionally, and spiritually balanced, then the general color of each chakra is predominately the one thought to be associated with it.

If you read different texts, you may find that they provide a different mineral and color classification for each of the chakras, such as turquoise for the crown chakra and amethyst for the root, as previously listed. Currently, the most popular associations appear to be the following:

Chakra	Color	Mineral
Root	Red	Ruby
Sacral	Orange	Coral
Solar plexus	Yellow	Topaz
Heart chakra	Green	Emerald
Throat	Blue	Turquoise
Third Eye	Violet	Amethyst
Crown	White	Quartz

The Minor Chakras

It is generally agreed that there are 21 minor chakras. Barbara Ann Brennan writes in *Hands of Light* that they are located as follows:

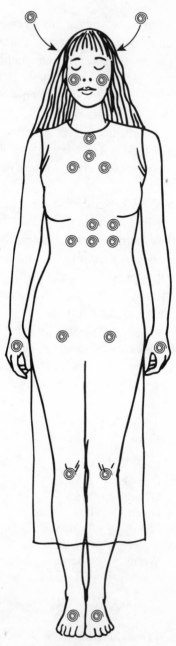

THE MINOR CHAKRAS

one in front of each ear (2), one above each breast (4), one where the collarbones meet (5), one on the palm of each hand (7), one on the sole of each foot (9), one above each eye (11), one on each gonad or ovary (13), one near the liver (14), one connected with the stomach (15), two connected with the spleen (17), one behind each knee (19), one near the thymus gland (20), and one near the solar plexus (21).

In addition, there is said to be 122 smaller, secondary chakras throughout the body.

Brennan and most other researchers are in agreement that all of these chakras, the major, the minor, and the secondary, are whirling vortices of energy, transmitting their individual energy from their tip to another through passageways located there. The point on the body where the tips of these chakras intersect is thought to correspond with many acupuncture points in traditional Chinese medicine.

Retained Memory

When we talk about how and where thought arises, most of us are referring to the processes that take place in our minds, in our brains. However, science has recently suggested that memory is not held in the mind or the brain but is held in the connective tissue, or the body's fascia.

These minor and smaller chakras are very important because they can become "trigger" points, a particular location on the body that holds and stores all our memories, particularly emotional pain and injury. These chakras can be used to locate and pinpoint areas locked in trauma, repetitive erroneous thinking, and emotionally overwhelming memories. A release of a painful trigger point can be done manually, but such a release is often temporary. A more permanent way to release these trigger points can be achieved by completing the tasks and exercises in the following chapters. This work will unblock the chakras and often will release painful trigger points and with it the painful memories that may be stored there. The release of trigger points and the resultant relief from pain that this unblocking can bring about is one method that can be used to diagnose whether or not the work of opening the chakras so energy can flow through has been accomplished.

Chakras Produce Your Aura

As the chakras spin, energized by the universe and the thoughts and emotions of each individual, each one generates its very own electromagnetic field, which combines with the electromagnetic fields generated by the other chakras to produce an auric field, or aura. The energy of each chakra at any given moment, as they combine their energies up and down the channel alongside the spine to produce your auric field, will determine what colors dominate in your aura. As they bring in energy from the universe, the colors shift as your emotions and thoughts vary. The colors they project as they blend and mingle create an ever-changing, ever-vibrant aura—one that is unique to each and every one of us.

4 The Aura: The Secret Messages Your Vibrations Send

Let your light so shine before men,
that they may see your good works.

—St. Matthew

The dictionary definition of an aura is an emanation or a radiation, a distinct but intangible quality that seems to surround a person or thing.

For more than five thousand years, in a time when the world was more accepting of things mystical, people spoke of the experience of seeing light or brilliant colors around the heads or surrounding the entire bodies of others. Thousands of years ago it was not rare for ordinary people to speak of seeing such energy. Through meditation or prayer, which was routinely a part of their lives, they heightened their sense of perception and thus expanded their consciousness so they were able to easily see halos or auras,

Auras Worldwide

Described as a shimmering nimbus or disk of colored light around the head, or a glowing luminous band of vibrant colors surrounding an individual, the aura has been mentioned in the literature of many cultures worldwide and depicted in their art. We have all seen religious paintings of saints and other sacred figures, their faces gleaming with a beatific light that has been cast upon them from the golden or colored shining light that surrounds them. Christianity has depicted Jesus, Mary, and numerous saints with halos of light above their heads or rays of light coming from their bodies. There are numerous biblical references to a luminous radiation surrounding individuals, such as Psalms (4:6) "Lord, lift up the light of Thy countenance upon us" or Matthew (17:2), who says that Jesus "was transfigured before them: and his face did shine as the sun and his raiment was white as the light." Ephesians (5:8) suggests that people "walk as children of light" and Acts (9:3) says, "and suddenly there shined around him a light from heaven."

Pictures of Buddha in Chinese and Japanese art often depict him as the Enlightened One with a halo surrounding his head, and Egyptian as well as Native American oral traditions describe a gleaming light enveloping or emanating from both people and animals.

Nostradamus

There is an oft-told story about Nostradamus, the physician and astrologer, who is best known for his book of prophecies, *Centuries,* written in the 1500s. Traveling down a narrow road, he stepped aside to let a group of Franciscan monks pass by. One young man was surrounded by such a beautiful glowing astral light that Nostradamus was brought to tears and fell to his knees in homage to Brother Felice Peretti, the young son of a swine herder. Years later, that same Franciscan brother was to be known as His Holiness, Pope Sixtus V, the pope who put the finances of the Papal States on a sound basis, rid the territory of bandits, encouraged the silk trade, and beautified Rome. Pope Sixtus V made the construction of a Vatican Palace and Library possible and was responsible for the completion of the dome of St. Peter's, designed by Michelangelo.

The Human Energy Field in Every Culture

It appears that every culture recognizes the existence of the human energy field and describes it. The Chinese structure their universe out of ever-changing energy that is known as *chi* or *qi*. East Indian religious beliefs are based on a human energy system of chakras that manifest themselves outside the body in the form of auras. Brazil, the Philippines, as well as most African cultures, base their spiritual practices on the concept that the human is composed of flowing energy that interacts with the universe.

John White, in his book *Future Science,* lists as many as ninety-seven cultures that, through the centuries and right up to the present time, refer to the phenomena of auras. Although people in these cultures discuss seeing such auras using a variety of words such as astral light, *chi, prana, karnaeem,* and *Illiaster,* they consider these visible energy fields surrounding living things to be quite normal and ordinary, and are quite surprised to learn that some people can't see them and don't believe in such things.

Those who say they can see auras describe them as a luminous glow that appears to surround every living thing with a constantly changing cloud of colors. Children often see auras, but we misunderstand them when they tell us that their teacher is green or that they saw a pink bear at the zoo. When they draw with crayons and make trees red and the sky yellow, they are corrected and told to color things the way adults tell them they really are. It is possibly this constant correction by adults who have lost their ability to see the aura that ultimately teaches children to disbelieve what their eyes tell them and causes them to also discard this natural skill.

While ancient traditions were not aware of the existence of energy fields or electromagnetic waves, they appear to have consistently described what science now says is the manifestation of the electromagnetic field that emanates from all animate matter and extends at least six inches and sometimes as much as five or six feet from the body.

Kirlian Photography

Although some people think that because they have not actually seen an aura, then auras do not exist or they exist only in the imagination, auras have been photographed in rigidly controlled

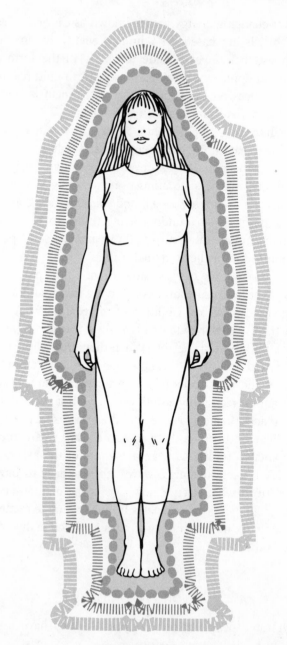

THE HEALTHY AURA

scientific experiments by a process known as Kirlian photography. This process photographs an object by exposing film in a dark room to ultraviolet light that results from electronic and ionic inter-actions caused by an electric field. It reveals a light, glowing band surrounding the person or the object. The theory is that the film records the subtle energy field that surrounds all forms of life, en-ergy that is not detectable by any ordinary processes. Although skeptics have maintained that aura photography is only the result of the moisture on the surface of the life form being photographed coming in contact with the photographic plate, Keith Wagner, a researcher at California State University, performed some experi-ments that disproved this theory. Wagner placed a Lucite block as a moisture barrier between the subject and the photographic plate and was still able to produce a Kirlian aura photograph.

The Auric Photograph

In 1980, an American engineer and inventor, Guy Coggins, devel-oped a camera that went beyond Kirlian photography; he claimed it could photograph the energy field around a human being. Others have also developed similar cameras and a variety of them are available for anyone interested in obtaining one. Variations of aura cameras are in use in over thirty-five countries worldwide at the present time.

According to Coggins, his camera produces a full-spectrum color representation of the aura. These photographs, when developed, show the upper half of the body and use traditional biofeedback measuring techniques, combined with high-voltage field imaging, to produce a electronic image of the aura of any individual.

Coggin's first aura camera measured the aura by transmitting radio waves through the subject via a hand plate. Then the com-puter converted the waves into electrical energy, which could be processed as light and color. While your photograph was being taken, you would place your hands on a probe that would send a radio frequency through your body and you would begin emitting radio waves at specific frequencies. The effect was to make your body a living antenna that relayed the information to a computer where it would be processed and displayed as electromagnetic energy—colors.

A number of researchers have experimented in the field of aura photography, including Dr. Hiroshi Motoyama of Japan, who worked with those whom he believed activated a specific chakra during meditation or spiritual practices, and Dr. Carlo Montanari, a biologist with a Ph.D. in medical statistics, who has taken over six thousand auric photographs and has been researching subtle energies in his lab in Milan, Italy.

Although still experimental, researchers in Russia have been working with spiritual healers, therapists, and others to collect thousands of photographs of people in differing states of emotion and physical health. They maintain that these films can provide information about the general state of tension or relaxation, as well as details about the emotional and physical health of any individual.

Also experimental, aura cameras are being used by chiropractors and others in alternative health to verify specific physical mental and emotional states in their patients. In conjunction with the various aura cameras, some of which are now being manufactured in a number of countries, including Russia, they then feed the photographic results into a computer. This computer prints out an interpretation of the color spectrum they have recorded. Because there are differing theories about the interpretation of what the colors in an aura mean, the jury is still out on whether such explanations are useful. Popular at fairs, shows, and expositions, these computer color analysis programs may be beneficial, or they may be no more than entertainment, such as the handwriting analysis or horoscope by computer that is often available at such affairs.

Quantum Physics

Quantum physics suggests that there are connections in the universe and dimensions of time and space that we do not as yet understand.

One thing that these quantum physicists have confirmed is that all matter is vibratory.

Dr. Valerie Hunt, a professor and researcher at UCLA, states emphatically, "The body is a flowing, interactive electrodynamic energy field."

Dr. Carlisle Holland, a osteopathic physicians, maintains that, "Our bodies are laid out like musical instruments. We are designed to vibrate and resonate."

You Have Experienced an Aura

While you may not as yet have visually experienced an aura, there is no doubt that, if you think about it for a moment, you will realize that you actually have experienced the aura of another person. You have *felt* an aura.

"He is so gloomy."
"He makes the hair stand up on the back of my neck."
"She's a little firecracker."
"He was green with envy."
"He's such a coward; he has a yellow streak down his back a yard wide."
"She is just feeling a little blue right now."
"I didn't trust him the first minute I saw him."
"Wow, he lit up like a Christmas tree!"
"Look at that face, he is glowing."
"I enjoy just being around her; she just radiates calm."
"She's a joy to be with."
"I'm in the pink!"
"I can't spend any time with him; it's a draining experience."
"I can't explain it, I really feel peaceful at her house."
"He's always so upbeat, so positive, he makes me feel like I can do anything."
"I can't tell you why, but I really don't like her."
"She always acts so cheery, but I feel like she is really sad inside."

"I hardly know her, but as soon as she comes in I want to
   leave."
"He has an aura of mystery about him."

I'm sure you recognize some of these statements—you may have
said some of them yourself or heard them said about others—or
maybe heard similar words or expressions used to describe you. If
you think about it, you may come up with many more that describe someone in a brief sentence, often using words with color
in them. What is being said here? The language is more than a simple description of the person; it is a vivid depiction of an aura, the
physical energy that emanates from a person that can be experienced or sensed by all who come into contact with that individual.

Auras Are in a Constant State of Change

In the study of color known as spectroscopy, the wavelengths of the
light emitted or absorbed by an atom or a molecule depend on
the structure and motion of the particles. When the vibration or rota-
tion of a molecule changes, the motion of its electrons also
changes, resulting in differing wavelengths of light being absorbed
or emitted. Subsequently, there is a change in the colors that each
molecule of energy projects.

Researchers have proposed theoretical models of auras based on
their frequencies and their vibratory rates. They have represented
them as existing around living matter in moving and flowing layers. Auras are in a constant state of change because their colors and
patterns flow and drift with every passing thought, action, and al-
teration in behavior. Every time you react to something, whether it
is physical, mental, or physical, your aura changes. The colors of
auras blend and merge as they fluctuate, and sometimes it is impossible to say exactly where one color begins and another ends.
Each person's aura is unique; no two are exactly alike because no
two people in the world are exactly alike, even identical twins.

However, with certain habitual modes of thinking and action,
there is usually a predominant appearance to each person's aura

and it is this overall feeling, the general sense of it and the person it represents, that most of us experience when we feel someone's aura.

The Layers of the Aura

Individual researchers have created a number of ways of describing the layers of the aura and most of them define the layers by location, color, brightness, density, fluidity, and function. Different researchers are interested in differing aspects of the aura—some with the physical, using the aura to diagnose illness; others with the spiritual or religious aspects; others with the psychological and emotional components. However, the majority of researchers conclude that there are most likely seven layers to the aura, with every other layer being highly structured in organized waves while the layers in between look like colored fluids that are constantly moving. These seven layers of an aura are said to correspond to the health or condition of every one of the major chakras. In other words, the first layer of the aura is associated with the first or root chakra, the second layer with the second chakra, and so on, through all seven chakras. As the chakra energy changes, the layers of the auras will flare out, sometimes blending, sometimes merging with different colors and hues, so that each individual, including you, is surrounded with an ever-changing, glowing ambiance that, to those nearby, will indicate exactly what kind of a person you are.

The first layer of the aura and the first chakra are associated with the function of your physical body. The second layer and the second chakra are linked with the pleasure aspects of your life. The third layer is bound to the balance and personal power you have. The fourth level and the fourth chakra are the vehicle for loving other people and humanity. The fifth level is allied to your ability to communicate, speak, and take responsibility for your actions. The sixth level is coupled with intuition and the ability to be creative, while the seventh level and the seventh chakra are connected with the spirituality and transcendence of your spirit.

Brennan, who states that she is able to observe these layers, writes that the first, third, fifth, and seventh layers appear to be scintillating, tiny lights, rapidly blinking at different rates, as if they have tiny electrical charges moving along them. The second, fourth, and sixth layers are fluid-like and only take on a structure as they flow through the others, while each succeeding layer interpenetrates all the layers under it, creating a glowing, gleaming, glittering field of energy that extends out beyond your physical body.

Layer One

The first layer of the aura, the one next to the physical body, is called the etheric body. Researchers such as Dr. John Pierrakos of the New York Institute for the New Age maintain that this layer of the aura shapes the physical body rather than the other way around. His work states that the web-like structure of this layer shoots off bluish-white sparks that twinkle like tiny holiday lights.

Layer Two

The second layer of the aura is known as the emotional body, whose colors include all the colors of the rainbow. These vary from clearly brilliant gradations to deep muddy colors, depending upon the energy and the emotions of the individual at the time. Displaying clouds or blobs of color in constant motion, the emotional body extends out beyond the first layer and often releases great bursts of color that mingle with the rest.

Layer Three

The third layer of the aura is known as the mental body and appears to be of even finer material. It emerges as a bright yellow light radiating from the head and shoulders and then enveloping the entire body, often expanding and becoming brighter and brighter as the individual concentrates. This yellow glow is infused with different globes of color when there is emotion attached to the thought, and when there is clear spiritual thought and transcendence. Thought and emotion forms the brilliant halo that has been seen around the upper body of holy individuals.

Layer Four

The fourth layer of the aura is known as the astral layer and it is made up of clouds of all the colors but is often infused with a rosy hue when it surrounds a loving person. When people fall truly in love, intuitives maintain that they can see great arcs of rose colored light passing from the heart of one person to another. This light shining from the heart is often see in portraits or statues of female saints holding a child.

Layer Five

The fifth layer of the aura is known by some as the blueprint, or template, layer and by others as the beginning of the outer shell. It creates an empty space, which then allows the other layers to take shape just as building the walls of a house then forms the interiors.

Layer Six

The sixth layer of the aura is known as the celestial layer and has a shimmering, opalescent glow that exists in everyone because it indicates each person's potential to become more ethical, more humane, more spiritual. It only shines like a beacon for those individuals who have actually made such a connection with the universe, who understand that all of humanity is linked, and who have made an effort to transcend their earthly passions.

Layer Seven

The seventh layer of the aura is known as the ketheric layer and it holds the entire structure of the aura together. It is shaped around the physical body with a glistening, sparkling web of light that is pulsating with energy. While the color associated with the seventh chakra is most frequently said to be white, this layer of the aura

ranges from a golden glow to a brilliant white, similar to that of the
after-burn of a rocket soaring into space, up to the cosmos.

The Rainbow of the Aura

The rainbow colors of the aura range through the spectrum from
violet to red, and these colors spark like flames. They move and
dance, they interweave, they flare and dim constantly as thoughts
pass through your mind, as emotions change, as ideas come and
go, as physical activity and energy levels ebb and flow.

The energy of the aura reflects itself in both light and color. The
color, its clarity, and its location at the moment all indicate different things about your physical, emotional, mental, and spiritual
well-being. Most experts believe that the colors nearest to the body
reflect physical conditions and energies and those farthest from the
body reflect emotional, mental, and spiritual energies. The clearer
and softer the colors, the better. Thick and muddy colors often reflect imbalances, while bright dark colors indicate high energy

Those who study auras and their colors have ascribed a variety
of meanings to the colors they present, which layer of the aura they
are in, and how they blend into one another. As we all know from
kindergarten, when different colors blend together a new hue is
formed, and when a darker color is added, the result is often
muddy. The flashing and flaring of color from the different layers
can result in a myriad of colors showing a variegated rainbow aura
to the world. The colors of the aura reflect the thinking of the individual at that moment and this can be felt by others, whether
they actually see any manifestation of it or not. These thoughts energize or block the various chakras, which, in turn, create the
energy that is the visible or felt aura.

Everyone is sensitive to colors. We have all admired a gorgeous
sunset or the sun sparkling off the blue water of a clear pool.
Everyone enjoys the calming effect of the green grass in a beautifully kept park, and the turning of the leaves in the fall is often the
occasion for people to make a long trip to the mountains to see

them at the height of their glorious oranges and red, which signal the beginning of autumn.

Some of us have favorite colors and other people associate particular colors with certain bad experiences. Mary won't wear a particular shade of blue any longer because that was the color of her dress when she was in an automobile accident. Hannah always wears her lucky yellow shirt to play bingo. A famous movie actress decorated her large Hollywood home entirely in pink, and some of today's country-western artists wear nothing but black. We've all had someone tell us we look great in a certain color or that sometimes we look washed out. These comments are often unconscious impressions, not of the clothes we are wearing, but of people's intuitive reading of our aura.

Auras change every moment. Every emotion, every thought, every mental activity can bring about both light and color fluctuations.

For those individuals who can see auras, learning to interpret the colors they observe can take a lifetime. For the rest of us, who usually feel or intuit the aura, the inability to actually see the colors in an aura is not important. However, as you think about your own chakras and your own aura, colors have a personal meaning. Later, as you work with the tasks for the various chakras, you might want to include some of these colors in your thoughts and in your daily life to reinforce your conscious beliefs about the changes you want to make.

Red—Root Chakra

In general, strong clear red is the color of fire and a primal creative force. It is connected to the earth with the smoldering heat of underground fires and volcanoes. It can be hot and primitive and can indicate strong passions, including the dynamic emotions of hate, anger, love, and change, as well as renewed life. Too much red can indicate overstimulation, inflammation, violent tempers, aggression, and impulsiveness.

To help protect and stimulate your root chakra, you might want to wear red shoes or red near your feet.

Orange—Sacral Chakra

A strong, brilliant orange is the color of warmth and creativity, courage, joy, and a mature sexuality. It is connected to the universe with the glow of both the warming sun and the pale cool color of the harvest moon. If the color is muddy, you may be prideful of your sexual prowess or too aware of your own masculinity or femininity for your own good.

If you wear orange clothing, similar to the brilliant orange robes worn by the monks of some Eastern religions, you are stimulating and protecting your primal creative force.

Yellow—Solar Plexus Chakra

Yellow, from the pale shades of new sunshine to the almost white of the outer tips of a sheaf of wheat, is the color of balance in your life as you harvest its rewards and optimism about the future seasons. It represents the centering of your psyche and the ability to be open to new learning opportunities and wisdom.

Deeper, muddier shades of yellow indicate feelings of being deprived of the recognition due you and excessive analyzing of others' behavior.

If you wear something yellow, you might protect and stimulate your enthusiasm for life.

Green—Heart Chakra

Green, from the almost black color of pine needles to the brilliant grassy green of the sun shining on a lawn, is the color of sensitivity and compassion. It represents opening your heart with sympathy to the love needs of others, as well as Nature's creatures, and a calm nature.

Dark green or muddy shades reflect uncertainty and miserliness, jealousy, possessiveness, and the inability to care about the emotions and woes of those less fortunate than yourself.

Wearing even a small sprig of green might help you to be reliable, dependable, and open to the heartfelt needs of others.

Blue—Throat Chakra

A pale blue of a summer sky, the ever-changing blues of an ocean as the tides and currents alter its surface, reflect the ability to communicate with others about what you want and also an understanding of what their words really mean when they talk to you. Deeper shades of blue are associated with loneliness, like a small sailboat on a great expanse of ocean. Royal blue is indicative of honesty in your speech and good judgment in what and whom you talk about.

The muddier shades of blue may indicate blocked perceptions of others' speech and a tendency to be domineering and oversensitive.

A touch of blue worn at the throat, such as a tie or scarf, may protect your ability to communicate honestly.

Purple—Third Eye Chakra

From the deep shades of eggplant to the palest of flowers, nature saves the color purple for some of its rarest beauties. Pale purple is the color of intuition and the power of ideas. It is a color of transmutation, for a blending of the heart and the mind, the physical with the spiritual. It reflects independence and the ability to see beyond the surface, to understand things as they really are.

Muddy purples reflect the need to overcome some of life's obstacles and perhaps indicate an erotic nature.

Sleeping on purple sheets may bring you intuitive answers to your questions about your life, as they can stimulate your dreams.

White—Crown Chakra

The wisp of clouds in the sky and a lovely white rose, tinged with pink, are the colors of truth and purity. White encompasses all colors and the auras of many saints and highly spiritual individuals glow brightly with a corona of white light edged in gold and pink.

White reflects a growing union with the universe and the awakening of the individual to a higher power and the yearning to connect with it. True spiritual energy and the ability to come into one's own power with enthusiasm and inspiration as an awakening takes place.

White curtains, white shirts, both will reflect the colors of the universe back to you and perhaps inspire you to greater heights as you journey through life.

Your Aura Is Your Life

Few of us actually claim to see the colors and the levels of the aura. The rest of us "feel" them.

The line "Laughing on the outside, crying on the inside" describes the social presentation that many of us make to the world. We are experts at presenting a very smiling and cheerful facade, while all the time suffering internally with depression, sadness, loneliness, and a variety of other emotions that we attempt to keep carefully hidden from view. However, your aura is your *true* presentation of yourself and try as you might, you cannot prevent that true self from shining through to those who are aware, grounded, and intuitive. Your aura is your actual physical, emotional, intellectual, and spiritual self, glowing and vibrating all around you. It is a presentation of yourself to the world that encompasses your entire well-being. It reflects how you live your life.

The colors of your aura and their vibrancy are changing moment to moment as your thoughts and moods change, but it is the overall presence of the aura that is felt and experienced by others. Your aura is your very own personal universe. Everything in your life is created *first* within your aura. It is not possible to create anything outside of yourself unless you begin by creating it within. If you think something won't work or that you are going to be disappointed in life or love, you are creating the climate for failure and disappointment within your aura and they will become manifest in reality.

The German scientist Julius Robert von Mayer and the British physicist James Prescott Joule formulated and proved a law of the conversation of energy that states, "Energy can neither be created nor destroyed, it can only be transformed." We have already examined quantum physics in relationship to chakras and auras and so we learn a very important lesson—*thoughts are energy*. Constant negative thinking is more detrimental than any of us can imagine. Continuously thinking that you don't deserve to be loved, that you are destined to only have lovers who hurt you, that you can't change the direction of your life is putting the kind of energy into your chakras that will activate an aura to surround you with negative energy, which can bring you those things that you really don't want!

Aura Viewing

Everyone has felt another person's aura, but you may think you have never seen one. If you are interested in increasing your ability to view auras, you may want to work with some of the following exercises to increase your aura intuition.

Number 1

Begin by thinking of someone you know quite well, who is not physically present at the moment.

Close your eyes and sit back. Be sure to relax your tongue because it is that tongue, always ready for self-talk, that will keep you from being totally calm.

Take a few very deep breaths from the diaphragm.

Create a mental picture of the person whose aura you want to see. (It might be your lover, your close friend, a relative. Try to see this person in your mind's eye as they were the very last time you were together. It helps if you can remember the person's clothing or conversation.)

> Does a color immediately come to mind in connection with this
> person? If you think:
> She was so sad the last time I saw her, so blue.
> He was laughing, feeling so warm and bright.
> Why does she always wear black?

You will know right away that you may be intuitively sensing the person's aura because that is what you are describing—their emotional state.

Whatever color you came up with when you thought of this person, visualize a big bubble of it completely surrounding them. Now mentally look at them through the bubble of color and focus on more detail. Concentrate. You may begin to see small wisps of color float by in the background. When you first see an aura, the main effect that you will get is of the person's physical health. The more symmetrical the radiations, the healthier the person. If there is a lack of symmetry, it indicates an imbalance of energy in the physical world. Other radiations will indicate moods and emotional states, as well as the individual's spiritual health, and these are usually seen as flares of color running through the overall color impression that you have of the person.

You will find that this intuitive aura, your visualization of someone at a distance, is usually quite accurate. With a little practice you may find that you are able to see someone's aura in your mind's eye quite easily.

Number 2

When you meet someone new, pay close attention to their appearance and the overall impression you get, and then later, when they are not there, try this mind's eye viewing. You may be surprised at what you can learn about someone when you are not taken up with the chatter and movement that distracts you when you are in their presence.

Auras are said to be the visible manifestation of energy fields. You can physically experience your own energy field in preparation to viewing it.

Sit relaxed in a comfortable chair, take a few deep breaths, focus your attention on your aura, and briskly rub your hands together.

Now cup your hands together, finger tips and heels of the palms of your hands almost touching. You will, of course, feel the warmth you generated by the friction of rubbing your hands together.

Close your eyes and concentrate on the feeling in your hands and fingers.

Very slowly separate your hands and feel the energy between them as you move them farther apart and then closer together, almost touching again. You may have the sensation that your hands are magnetized and when you move them to within a couple of inches of each other, you can feel resistance.

Perform this exercise several times during the day and you will become aware of your own energy shifts as your energy field expands and contracts along with your own emotional states. With practice, you can begin to feel your own energy field changing as your mood and energy changes. There will be times when you can feel the energy in your own hands when they are as far apart as six inches and at other times, it will be necessary for your fingertips to be almost touching for you to feel anything.

Nurses who practice therapeutic touch say that, with practice, they can feel the energy in their own hands, and it has a variety of subtle differences or tones. At different times it may feel dense, flowing, tingling, vibrating, bubbling, or even like a small electric shock.

Practice feeling your own energy field expanding and contracting so that you are aware that it is there and then you may be ready to try to see your own aura.

Number 3

Individuals who regularly see auras report that they are seen with the peripheral or side vision rather than with the central part of the vision. If you want to see an aura, you are more likely to do so if you glance at the person from the side of your eyes rather than looking or staring directly at them. The simple explanation is that the cells in your eyes known as the rods are sensitive to low levels of light rather than the bright light of daytime, so to see auras you need to use the rod cells rather than the cone cells, which are used in bright light.

We have all been taught to focus directly on something we want to see. If you want to read a book, see where you are going as you drive down the streets, have a conversation with someone, you usually look directly at them with your central vision, using the cone cells. In order to release the dominance your central vision has over how you look at things, you may have to practice so that you can learn to let your peripheral vision take over.

Look straight ahead and then extend your arm in front of your face with your index finger pointing toward the sky. Keeping your arm extended, slowly move your arm to the right while you continue to look straight ahead. Note where your field of vision ends because this is where your peripheral vision begins. This is where you will see an aura.

Number 4

Sit relaxed in a comfortable chair, take a few deep breaths, center yourself, and lean forward, resting your arms on your knees with your hands hanging freely from the wrists. Slowly bring your fingertips together in front of you until your index fingers are touching each other very lightly.

Without blinking, gaze at a place on the floor just beyond where you can see your fingers touching. Using the kind of unblinking stare we often employ when we daydream, soften your focus (this will blur your vision slightly) and slowly separate your fingertips until they are about one inch apart.

Gaze without blinking at the area on the floor that you can see just between your fingertips. Begin, very slowly, to move your fingers slightly apart, closer together and then apart again.

You may have to practice several times, but after a while you will see little smoky trails that appear to be connecting your fingertips to each other. These are tiny wisps of energy. You are looking at your own aura! An aura is a very ephemeral thing, so don't expect to be able to examine it or gaze at for any length of time. It may flash, pulsate, and then vanish before you can really be sure you saw it, because that is the nature of auras.

If you continue to practice, you may begin to see that this mist of energy has color. As you become aware of the color, you will find that it changes as your energy field changes because you are moving from one level of consciousness and awareness to another.

If you become comfortable seeing your aura as it is visible between the tips of your fingers, practice the same with your hands and your forearms. Bring them together and then separate them, looking for this smoky mist or trail between them.

Be patient. Practice. You can see your own aura.

Number 5

When you have practiced observing the energy field that is traveling between the parts of your own body—fingertips, knees, forearms—you are ready to attempt to view your own aura in total.

Stand in front of a mirror in very soft light, similar to twilight. Viewing will be easier if the background is one solid color. You can always hang a plain white towel against the wall behind you if necessary. Take a deep breath and soften your focus. Look into the mirror over your own shoulder at a place on the wall behind you. Your own reflection should be visible just on the edge of your peripheral vision. Try not to blink, but if you must, keep the same soft dreamy focus. Don't let your ego get involved. You are not there to look at yourself in the mirror but to see the pale smoke that is clinging to your skin. Do this exercise for a few moments and then let go because if you try to force it, you will lose that dreamy focus. You might also try adding something stimulating—music, holding a crystal, or adding some perfume to the air. Even subtle changes to the environment can affect your aura because it responds very quickly to changes in your emotions and moods.

Number 6

You might try practicing on a plant or on your pet if you have one. Cats are very sensitive to someone looking at their aura and if you stare, you may find that your cat will move away from you, because your projected energy has made it uneasy.

Number 7

If you want to view another person's aura, it is done in the same manner. It is much easier to look at someone you are not directly in contact with, so try doing so as you sit on the grass at the park or along the sea wall at the beach.

Again, take some deep breaths, soften the focus of your vision, and gaze just over the shoulder of the person. You should be able to see the same wisps of smoke around his or her head or along the side of the head and shoulder.

Once you have seen the aura emanating from your own fingertips or from the head or shoulders of another person, you should have little difficulty accepting that auras do exist. Until you fine tune your auric vision, you will see a mist that is colorless, but if you continue to practice you should begin to see some color, flaring and scintillating around any living thing.

Aura Goggles

Some New Age shops and bookstores sell aura goggles and some people find them useful. These glasses are made with colored lenses—orange, blue, purple, and so forth. The theory is that they have an effect on the sensitivity of the rods in your eye and will speed up your ability to see auras. If you have some sunglasses with colored lenses, you might try viewing auras through them. Doing so might help you begin to see the aura more rapidly.

Keep Chakra Energy Circulating

Many people who can see auras believe that it is essential to keep your chakra energy circulating within your own body so that your aura stays strong and vital. We have all seen photos of yogis sitting with their legs in the lotus position and the tips of their thumbs and index fingers on each hand touching each other. Centuries of practice have taught them that this posture is beneficial because it is a method of keeping their energy from being dissipated.

When you are feeling low, as if your energy is draining away, or you feel in need of recharging, you might try this Buddhalike position. If you find this position difficult or too strenuous, you might try sitting with the palms of your hands touching and both of your feet flat on the ground, connecting to the energy of the earth. Breathe deeply, close your eyes, and concentrate on bringing the energy of the universe into your body and up and down your spine. You will find that this is relaxing, balancing, and grounding.

If you doubt that your energy can be changed by your thoughts, you might try an experiment used by some QiGong masters when they wish to prove to those who doubt that thoughts can visibly alter *qi*.

In a standing position, hold both arms out in front of your body with your hands at the level of the third eye. Place one hand on top of the other, keeping the elbows straight. Try to keep your thinking neutral and then have a friend press down with one hand on your hands for a steady count of five. This is not a test of the strength of either individual, but it is for both of you to discover the amount of force your friend needs to exert and for you to see the strength you need to resist a steady pressure on your hands.

Now repeat the same test with the same position of the hands and the same amount of pressure from your friend. This time say in your mind, with great conviction, "*I am strong.*"

Repeat the test a third time, but say in your mind, "I am *not really* very strong."

Most people who perform this test without any preconceived desire for it to go one way or the other will be able to feel the differences in their strength and will appear weaker to anyone observing the test, even though no words are spoken out loud. This very simple test shows how we can be governed by our thoughts. You not only change your posture and your strength with the change in your thinking, you alter the energy flow through your chakras and into your aura.

Change Your Thoughts to Change Your Reality!

If you constantly dwell on life's problems, thinking that you will never meet someone to love, that things will never get better for you, you are setting the stage for a self-fulfilling prophecy.

If you wish to change your aura and your future, then you must change what and how you think. You must bring out from your unconscious into your conscious mind an awareness of all the aspects of how you live—feelings, reasoning, flexibility, responsibility, self-expression, creativity, diet, exercise, and spiritual practices. You may find areas of your life where you are numb or are avoiding the pain certain experiences and memories have caused you, because examining that pain means you would have to do something about it, and that is always very difficult.

When you have examined how you live with whom you choose to associate, and how you want to change, and then altered those elements that contribute to a lack of color and vibrancy in your aura, you will have an aura that is whole and healthy. Changing your thinking and your reality will produce chakras that are no longer blocked but are cleansed and cleared, rotating fully, aligned and functioning, providing energy to an aura that is truly representative of a balanced energy field. You will be an individual who is aware, self-confident, and mindful of your true self.

Perhaps you now wonder how to change your energy flow. You may find that if you concentrate on particular areas of your body, where the chakras are located, and focus on change or the direction you want your life to go, it is difficult to maintain concentration as you go about your daily tasks. You might remember to think about these things for a moment or two, but then the telephone rings, someone speaks to you, or you need to concentrate on your work, and the moment and the thought are gone.

It will become obvious that you need to set aside a few moments to concentrate on this task, and that special time is called meditation. The dictionary definition of *meditation* is "to ponder, reflect, or muse." You will need to set aside a brief period, some time during your day, to ponder or reflect—to the exclusion of other activities. For thousands of years people have found meditation to be a way to gain calmness and insight. As a meditator you will create a new pattern of neurological response because researchers have demonstrated that longtime meditators actually beneficially rewire their brain's circuitry. Meditation will shut down some of the excessive activity of the logical side of your brain, the left hemisphere, and allow the right side of your brain, the creative side, to come into balance. Thus, meditating will affect your chakra energy and, ultimately, your aura.

As a meditator you should set aside a quiet place where you can pause, breathe deeply for a few moments, relax, and focus your thoughts on the information you have discovered about yourself. With this calm creativity you will draw material out of your subconscious into your conscious thought and ultimately this will change and strengthen your aura.

For those who have not meditated before, you may need a little patience and effort to begin. Just the thought of setting aside time to be quiet and alone is difficult for many people because they have never learned how to really relax. When questioned, some say that they think people who meditate are a little odd or very religious or different from themselves. However, it is an age-old custom that has been shown to be beneficial to millions of people. As you try to meditate, set aside a small area of your house and place some candles there (because gazing at the center of a flame is a helpful meditation focus for many) or certain objects that help you focus on the colors you want to bring into your aura, such as a ribbon or a brightly colored shell.

Although you may have been taught that the left side of the brain is the logical side and the right side the creative side, in actuality the hemispheres of the brain are integrated and both sides are in constant use by everyone. Neurological studies of the brain waves of meditators show that meditation can actually improve the balance of the two hemispheres, making the person feel better, calmer, more insightful, and more able to face his or her daily life.

Relaxation

In order to meditate, you need to be able to relax. If you have difficulty doing so, the following relaxation technique has been used by many pain clinics throughout the United States to encourage their clients to learn to take it easy in a very short period of time.

- Lie comfortably on your back on the floor with your eyes closed. Begin by inhaling, tensing one leg, and raising it a few inches off the ground. Hold for a few seconds and then let it drop heavily down as you exhale. Repeat with the other leg.
- Inhale deeply and tense the muscles of one arm as you raise it a few inches off the ground. Hold for a few seconds, then let it drop heavily down as you exhale. Repeat with the other arm.
- Inhale deeply and tense the muscles of your buttocks as you raise your pelvis a few inches off the floor. Hold for a few seconds and then let it drop as you exhale.
- Inhale deeply and push your stomach out like a balloon. Hold for a few seconds and relax your stomach as you exhale.
- Inhale deeply and hold that breath with your chest expanded for a few seconds. Relax as you exhale.
- Inhale deeply and bring your shoulders up toward your ears, bring them together in front of you, and push them down toward your feet, relax, and exhale.
- Inhale deeply and squeeze all the muscles of your face tightly. Hold for a few seconds and relax as you exhale.
- Bring your thoughts to your breathing. Breathe with your diaphragm and slowly breathe deeper with each breath.

After you have practiced this technique a few times, you may find that you can stop whatever activity you are engaged in, inhale deeply, and tense all your muscles at once. Hold for a few seconds and relax as you exhale. Try it anytime you feel tense; you may find doing so helps you to feel better at those moments during the day when everything is going wrong and you feel the tension creeping into your neck and shoulders.

Suspend Disbelief

As you begin to work with the exercises and the tasks in this book, at first you may have to suspend a sense of disbelief. You may think that chakras and auras aren't real, that the suggested exercises are just fun, like one of those quizzes we have all taken in the women's magazines, and they actually won't make any difference. You may be tempted skip around and only work on the ones you think you can readily apply to yourself. Don't give in to this temptation because in reality, the exercises that you wish to avoid or that you scoff or laugh at are the very ones that can get to the heart of the problems with your relationships. Do them all and do them in order. You will find, as you experience this process, that things will begin to change—you will change and situations and people around you will change. You will be a witness to your own renewal program in progress.

You may use this book as a workbook, write in it, and use the margins to make notes to yourself, because many thoughts will crop up—old memories, some pleasant, some painful, and anecdotes of experiences you have had that verify your thinking, thoughts that point to the way you want your life to go now, or thoughts that you may want to review again.

Perhaps you will find that as you go through this process, you will also experience emotional highs and lows. You may find yourself feeling frustrated, frightened, depressed, amused, irritated, or sad. You may think, "Boy, have I been a fool," or feel that you have been an idiot, trod upon, or used, or even perhaps that you have been a user, a manipulator—all sorts of things that now add up to regret. However, keep in mind that whatever experiences in your past have prompted you to make changes your life, you now want to experience the hope and renewal that made you decide to read this book and do the work in the first place.

Let the Universe Help You

Finally, as you complete the work, you will have a new sense of yourself, an increase in self-esteem and a commitment to making your life better. You will learn where you took the wrong fork in the road, you will discover how to nurture yourself, to protect yourself from the same kind of errors in the future, to use those old painful scars to find a new direction; to go forward with new goals, wishes, and dreams, hopefully into a nurturing relationship, with a strong aura—healed.

There is much power in the universe, waiting to flow into your chakras, energize your aura, and help you improve your life. Open yourself up to this limitless, abundant source of the things you need: guidance, nurturing, and love. Ask for it and then take it in, because as you change your thinking, the universe will provide you with exactly what you seek. Thinking about what you need to do to change your attitudes, emotions, and beliefs is the first step toward creating the answer to your quest, because then the universe will bring it to you. Trust the universe because its energy is not chaotic. It is there for you to tap into like a benevolent friend.

5 Heal Who You Are Within the Universe

Truly great people emit a light that warms
the hearts of those around them.

—B. Yoshimoto
Japanese writer b. 1968

If you've seen a lot of movies, some romantic, some not; if you've read a lot of novels, some joyously romantic and some with unhappy endings for the lovers; or if you've watched an ongoing TV series and followed the ups and downs of those relationships week after week, you already know that a lot of us, on the pages of books, on the screen, and in real life, have fallen in love with the wrong person, at the wrong time, for the wrong reasons.

If you are determined to make better choices and to avoid repeating the same mistakes, then perhaps it is time to examine some areas of your life and your loves that you never gave any thought to before.

The first, or root, chakra, which is located at the base of the spine, is considered the grounding chakra, the one that connects you to the earth and is the manifestation of your unique life force. It is a building block and the foundation of all the other chakras The root chakra provides your grounding energy for survival. Its element is the earth and all it represents: your body, your survival, and your material and financial needs, including the ability to focus on and bring forth the things that will satisfy those needs. It is where you express your feelings of being connected to the universe and serves as the foundation for your understanding of all earthly experiences, those that are solid, stable, and tangible.

When people speak of someone being "grounded," we all know that the meaning is not punishing a teenager by confining him to the house. We understand that when we speak of someone as being "grounded," someone who "has their feet firmly planted on the ground," we are talking about a person we can rely on, someone we can trust to not sway or be toppled by the winds of change. We know they are reliable; they have a stability, a literal connection to their place on the planet in such a way that they are secure, steady, and balanced.

A person with a weakly grounded root chakra will not be able to focus on stability—in relationships, in careers, in life's goals. If your root chakra is blocked, tilted, or even temporarily low in energy, you may find yourself attracted to cults or strong leaders, or perhaps lovers and friends who are energetic and exciting, who seem charismatic in the beginning but who eventually manipulate you for their own purposes. These charismatic relationships can be blindingly seductive, alluring, and thrilling—until it is too late, and you end up being hurt and feeling abandoned, used, and sadly disappointed.

A strong first chakra will help change that and bring those who are balanced and secure into your life, people who are not manipulative, who are well grounded themselves, with stable jobs and other relationships, friends and lovers you can be proud to know and have in your life.

When we feel unloved or unworthy of being loved, it is very easy to find a lot of reasons to be negative about ourselves. The following exercises and small tasks will help you examine some of your fundamental beliefs and how you view your place in the world. As you explore your thinking, you will actually alter your root chakra. Small things, such as those as suggested in the tasks, may seem unimportant or trivial, but as you perform them, you will find that just thinking about them assists you in elevating your self-esteem, altering and strengthening your power, and thus stimulating your aura to glow and brighten. The very process of thinking about the answers to these quizzes will bring unconscious behavior up to your consciousness and those thoughts will become energy, which will transform the vigor of your chakras and animate your aura.

Don't jump ahead and read the quiz questions, but answer each one before moving on to the next. You should be honest with your answers, instead of wondering how you will appear to the person looking over your shoulder when you have finished. This is meant to be a learning process that will assist you in identifying your strengths and weaknesses by bringing into your consciousness some of the unconscious material that may be keeping you in a negative love relationship.

Your Role Model—Part A

1. Write the name of someone you admire, someone you think of as a role model. Don't spend a lot of time pondering whom to select. Make your selection quickly and write the name of the first person who comes to mind. _____

2. Now answer the following questions about your choice:
   a. Is this person living today?   Yes___   No___
      If you chose someone who is no longer living, write a brief sentence describing why you selected this individual.

      _____

      _____.

   b. Is your choice well known, a historical figure, a celebrity?
      Yes___   No___
      If you selected someone well known or a celebrity, write a brief sentence about why you selected this individual.

      _____

      _____.

   c. Is your choice someone you know personally?
      Yes___   No___

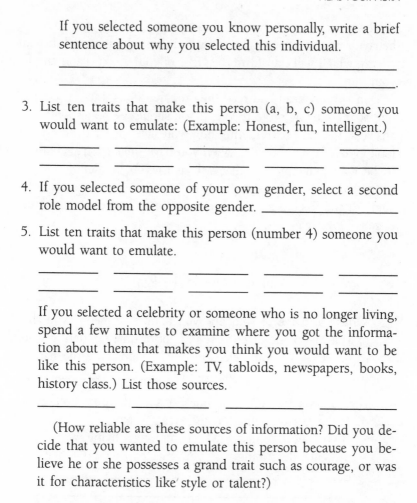

If you selected someone you know personally, write a brief sentence about why you selected this individual.

_____

_____.

3. List ten traits that make this person (a, b, c) someone you would want to emulate: (Example: Honest, fun, intelligent.)

_____   _____   _____   _____   _____

_____   _____   _____   _____   _____

4. If you selected someone of your own gender, select a second role model from the opposite gender. _____

5. List ten traits that make this person (number 4) someone you would want to emulate.

_____   _____   _____   _____   _____

_____   _____   _____   _____   _____

If you selected a celebrity or someone who is no longer living, spend a few minutes to examine where you got the information about them that makes you think you would want to be like this person. (Example: TV, tabloids, newspapers, books, history class.) List those sources.

_____   _____   _____   _____

(How reliable are these sources of information? Did you decide that you wanted to emulate this person because you believe he or she possesses a grand trait such as courage, or was it for characteristics like style or talent?)

Now look over your answers. Do you find that you relied on information from others, such as books, television, and friends, rather than actually knowing this individual and seeing his or her actions for yourself?

Mr. or Ms. Right

6. Write the name of your most recent or current significant other.

_____

7. On one side of the page, write at least five traits of this person you admire. On the other side, list at least five qualities he or she possesses that you dislike.

    _____   _____

    _____   _____

    _____   _____

    _____   _____

    _____   _____

8. Write the names of all of your previous significant others, include anyone you had a relationship with that you thought was meaningful; be sure to include any relationship that, for whatever reason, didn't last long.

_____   _____   _____   _____

9. For each name on the list, write at least five traits of this person that you admired. On the other side list at least five qualities they possessed that you disliked.

    _____   _____

    _____   _____

    _____   _____

    _____   _____

    _____   _____

When you first meet someone attractive, it's easy to see what you like about them. Not only are they on their best behavior, but you usually don't discover their flaws until you have known them for a while. If, as you look over these lists, you find that you often chose a significant other for a particular trait, you may realize that something you thought unimportant in the beginning eventually turned out to be very important as the relationship grew. (For example: If you list a trait such as "enthusiasm" for several of your past loves, as a characteristic you found attractive in the beginning, and then you list "unable to follow through on projects" as one of the things you dislike at the end of the relationship, you need to examine carefully how you can judge a person's enthusiasm more realistically. (For example: Pick out one of the interests he or she mentioned in your first couple of meetings. Just how long did the person stay interested in that enthusiasm before moving on to the next one?)

10. Go over your list of significant others. Write down how long you knew each person before the situation became what you would consider a "relationship." If you knew this person for less than twelve months, you didn't really know him or her; you just wanted to think you did. Today, people often jump right into a physical relationship, accepting that kind of intimacy as just a regular and expected part of dating behavior. It takes courage to go against the current way of thinking, but perhaps this is why people really do not get to know each other. If you have the courage to wait until you have spent time communicating together before you commit to a physical relationship, it may be possible to avoid the disastrous consequences and the emotional pain that results from not looking before you leap.

11. Now go back over this list, starting at Item 8, and at the end of the "dislike" column write a short description of why this relationship came to an end. Never mind the complicated details of the breakup, the misunderstandings, or the last dispute. Never mind who was to blame or that your heart was broken, find a phrase that is the truth about what caused the end. If he was too critical or you were too domineering; if she was too obsessive or he was too selfish, say so. When you have finished your list, if you see something repeated more than once, that should be a clue about what might go wrong in your next relationship. (Example: If you can't handle criticism but that is what proved disastrous in your previous relationships, you need to observe a potential partner for a while to see if this person is very critical of others because the problem might not just be the other person. You also need to think about the opposite of critical—see whether you are too sensitive. Now perhaps you can see an area in your behavior that you need to work on. Perhaps you need to face the fact that you have dif-

ficulty accepting criticism before entering into another relationship where this identical dynamic could again be played out.)

Your Role Model—Part B

1. List the most significant individual from your childhood who filled the role of father for you (father, stepfather, foster parent, grandfather, uncle). What is the first word that you think of when you think of him? _____

    List the first five positive and five negative traits of this father figure that come to your mind.

    _____   _____
    _____   _____
    _____   _____
    _____   _____
    _____   _____

2. List the most significant individual from your childhood who filled the role of mother for you (mother, stepmother, foster parent, grandmother, aunt). What is the first word that you think of when you think of her? _____

    List the first five positive and negative traits of this mother figure that come to your mind.

    _____   _____
    _____   _____
    _____   _____
    _____   _____
    _____   _____

3. When you think of the relationship between these two people, write five items that describe it. You are describing their interaction now, not character traits. (For example, if your father was in charge in the relationship and your mother was accepting when it came to decision making, write: he: controlling—she: passive.)

    _____   _____   _____   _____   _____

Examine what you wrote in Part A.

If the person you chose for a role model is a celebrity or a famous figure from history, someone who is really unknown to you but you read about them in a history book or saw them on TV, examine whether you have simply created a *fantasy* person, someone who looks good, sounds good, earns a lot of money, or has what appears to be an exciting life, someone you can never be like because you admire them for a particular special skill, rather than someone with ethical character traits that you can strive to emulate. Perhaps you selected someone like a basketball player because he is very talented, without actually knowing anything about how he conducts his personal life.

Is it possible that, in the past, you also selected a relationship with a *fantasy* lover? It is very easy to see someone who is physically appealing and then create a personality for him or her wishing such a gorgeous person would be all the things you long for, instead of looking beyond the facade and seeing the person inside. If you are not tuned in to others' auras, if you accept at face value, you need to understand that learning to see beyond the facade takes time.

If you selected a role model for character traits, you may find that you chose someone to admire and emulate who has qualities you lack yourself. If you have done that, then you need to look at these qualities to discover what you want to improve in yourself.

Examine what you wrote in Part B.

Whether we like it not, these are the people, our parent figures, who are our real role models, the ones from whom we learn how our gender behaves in this culture and how we should behave when we relate to others. We all know about nature and nurture—that is, one aspect of who we are is what we were born with, our genetics; and part of who we become, our nurturing, is due to what happens to us throughout our lifetime. Of course, peers and siblings play a role in everyone's development, but our parents demonstrate to us the standards of behavior.

Examine all the exercises you have completed so far.

Look for any repetitive words and circle them.

Do you see *trustworthy, true, valid, honest, faithful, reliable,* or *authentic* there? If the word *trust* does not appear in some form, then you absolutely will have a problem in any current relationship, and you may expect to have the same problem in future ones. Now that you have seen that *trust,* the absolute basic ingredient in any relationship, is missing, you can work on it. You can begin by being reliable, honest, and authentic yourself while you generate the vibrations that you expect such ethical conduct from others, too. As you do, the health of both your root chakra and your relationships will improve.

If you find that words such as *dishonest, unreliable, irresponsible, liar, cheat, submissive, obsessive, critical,* and *hysterical* appear, you may realize just what kind of relationships you have not only allowed to take place, but have unconsciously sought, because they filled emotional voids and satisfied negative needs learned years ago.

Friends

Answer the following questions:

1. Do you have friends from your childhood you either see or speak to?   Yes___   No___
2. Do you have friends from post-high school you either see or speak to?   Yes___   No___
3. Name the one person you consider your closest friend. _____.
4. Do you currently have five female friends whom you could ask to help you in an emergency?   Yes___   No___
5. Do you currently have five male friends whom you could ask to help you in an emergency?   Yes___   No___
6. Do you stay in touch with your parents?   Yes___   No___
7. Do you stay in touch with any of your siblings? Yes___   No___

8. Is there a place, other than where you live now, that you think
   of as home?   Yes___   No___   If yes, name it. _____
   When was the last time you went there? _____

The root chakra is our connection to the earth and to others. If
you have lost touch with old friends, if you don't have friends who
would help you in an emergency, you may need to work on re-
newing or strengthening some of these relationships because it will
fortify your survival skills as you find the messages your past can
bring forth from your memories. This is information about the primal you, which is so essential to understanding your beginnings
and your individuality.

Michael

At first Michael, a thirty-two-year-old CPA, said he didn't have any
role models that he could think of. He admired a number of sports
figures and he laughed at the suggestion that any of his teachers
could serve as a role model for him. Finally, Michael selected
Charles Lindbergh, the famous aviator who made the first solo
flight across the Atlantic in the late 1920s. Michael said, "He was
an adventurer, he had a lot of courage because he was willing to
try something that had never been done before. I guess he was a
thrill seeker and I would really like to be like him. I think I am
too cautious most of the time."

He selected Madonna as his other gender role model and he
laughed about that choice. "At first I thought I chose her because
she is very, very rich and has a 'take no prisoners' attitude when it
comes to advancing her career. But as I thought about it a little
more, I really do think Madonna is brave. She was willing to take
chances with her career and her life. And, although I didn't approve of some of the things she did—like that sex book of hers
that created such an uproar and having a baby and then dumping
the father—I think overall it appears both her life and her career

have taken a lot of courage. I got all this information from TV and the tabloids. I really don't know her."

On Michael's lists about his current relationship with Patti, and in the past with Ann and Sarah, he had listed "pushy" for all of them. "Wow," he said, "I'm amazed, I really thought they were all very different. I am attracted to women who are forthright and honest. I really don't care for shallow girls who are only interested in clothes and make-up. Now I realize that what I saw at first as being forthright often turned out to be a not very attractive form of aggressiveness that I would call pushy. I thought they were being honest when they spoke up for themselves, told me what they wanted."

Michael laughed. "When what they wanted wasn't what I wanted, I guess that is when assertive turned into pushy."

The other thing Michael had not observed was that his own lack of courage or fear of risk taking was being balanced by the aggressive behavior of his girlfriends. Michael needed to strengthen his root chakra so that he would not continue to allow himself to be dominated in relationships by such energetic, dynamic women.

Judith

Judith's family moved and lived in several small towns in Illinois before she graduated from high school. In the summer right after her graduation she moved to Chicago.

"Everybody in my high school couldn't wait to get out of that one-horse town and head for the big city. We wanted excitement and bright lights and the kinds of glamorous jobs that didn't exist in a small town." Although she went back at the holidays for the first few years, she gradually found that her life was too busy to visit every year and most of the people she knew from high school had moved away, too.

"I just quit going back. My parents are still there, but I found them so narrow-minded and boring that it was almost too painful for me to visit them. My mother just talked about her vegetable garden and quilting, while Dad talked about his dogs and what the guys down at the Legion Hall have to say about the government." She paused. "I guess they found my visits painful, too, because they weren't calling too often to see if I planned to visit."

When Judith finished the Friends exercise, she said that she just sat there and cried. "I suddenly realized there isn't any place I consider home, someplace I could go back to and feel safe and welcome. After Chicago, I moved to Milwaukee and then to Atlanta. These were moves I made because I felt I could do better in my career, make more money, find new and exciting friends. But the reality of it is that if a relationship soured, I'd find an excuse to move, and once I moved on, I didn't stay in touch with any of the people in Chicago or Milwaukee. If I left Atlanta today, it would just be the same. I know lots of people but I don't really *know* them. Most of them are people I met at work and maybe had a drink with occasionally, but nobody I could really consider any more than an acquaintance."

Judith smiled sadly, "I've had a couple of really hot romances but they cooled down just as fast as they heated up. The last one was a real bad experience. He was a charming guy, but he borrowed money from me all the time. He'd pay it back and then borrow again, but each time the amount he needed was larger. I loaned him several thousand dollars the last time I saw him and now I don't know where he is.

"I've laughed at girls I worked with who would come in all excited about some new guy they just met and they would say things like, 'He's so energetic, I just love a high-energy man,' or 'He has this great dry cleaning business, I just know he's going to be rich,' or 'He plays the guitar and he says he's going to write a song just for me.' Right away, they would decide they were in love, begin seeing him every night, and it didn't take long for them to fall into bed, saying it was love. I knew they were just fantasizing about these men, turning some minor attribute into a reason for a relationship. I dreaded the day I'd be listening to their sad stories about how these men didn't turn out to be anything they thought they were. Then I had my little fling with the bum who borrowed money and never paid me back, and I realized that I had done the very same thing. It is so easy to see what is happening with somebody else's relationship, even people you don't know very well, people who think they are falling in love for all the right reasons while you know they are starting a relationship for some silly, nonsensical reason with the wrong person.

"I don't have any friends I can confide in. I'm not like the ones I work with who tell everybody within earshot all the details of their lives. There is always a reason, like just moving on, being bored and changing jobs, to account for why I don't have any real friends I can call on in an emergency. Oh, I guess somebody at work would give me a ride if my car broke down, but I can't think of anybody I could ask to do much more than that. When I had to name my best friend, I thought of a girl in my class in high school—and then I had to get my yearbook out to spell her last name. How's that for a best friend?"

"I never tried meditation, but I liked the idea of making a special little niche in my bedroom. I set up a little end table with candles on it in the colors of all of the chakras, with a red one at the very center. I sat on the floor in front of them, lit all the candles, said my little root chakra affirmation, and thought about my life. I focused on my root chakra because I realized I didn't feel like I had any stability in my life. I had started to feel like I was just roaming the earth, looking for love. After a few weeks I began to feel a little better for no particular reason that I could name, but I found that my parents were frequently in my thoughts."

Judith realized that not only did she feel she had no connection to the place she was living now, she had missed establishing any roots.

"I decided to go home to visit my parents, but I made plans to stay for my entire vacation, two weeks, instead of just a couple of days. I always thought of my mother as so matronly and old because she is a little heavy, but actually she is only twenty years older than me. During the first week I worked in the garden with my mother and I was amazed at what she knew about planting and stuff, what good physical shape she was in to do all the heavy yard work, and she was so thrilled to have me kneeling on the ground beside her, she just couldn't stop talking. I didn't realize it, but they grow everything they eat, except for things like flour and sugar, right there in their own backyard. I felt the ground under my knees for the first time in years, I looked at the trees and the grass, and I felt cradled, nourished.

"Then later I sat at the kitchen table with my Dad while he fixed something, I think it was an old toaster, and I realized that all my life he was always busy working with his hands. I looked at the old beat-up piece of metal he held and I felt the rungs of the kitchen chair pressing against my back. That chair has been in their kitchen as long as I can remember. I felt so at home and peaceful. He told me stories about what he had done in the service, when he was in the Navy. I was never interested in it when I was a kid. He's had a very interesting life and I now realize that my parents are very happy living simply and quietly. They are connected to their community and do a lot of things for their neighbors and friends. Their only sorrow has been that I was too busy trying to be sophisticated to see them as they really are.

"I walked around town with Dad and we went into the hardware store and there was one of the guys I remember from high school working there. I was so glad to see him I almost cried. I guess he was glad to see me, too, because he called to ask me to dinner at his parent's house. I don't know if anything will come of it, but I know that this is someone who comes from the same background as I do, and that is a very different start for a relationship than I've ever experienced before.

"When I go back to Atlanta, I just don't know what will happen but I realize that I've started on a new journey, a new adventure, one that isn't about looking for excitement but for stability."

It was easy for Judith to realize that her root chakra was out of balance and by thinking about grounding herself and uniting with her family, she has begun to make changes in her thinking and her life that could be essential to her survival.

Thoughts = energy. What you think, you become.

Root Chakra Tasks

As you examine the areas of your life that are governed by your root chakra, you may wish to set aside a little time and a special place so that you can meditate and visualize about the changes you want to make in your life.

Select a red candle and light it, as you visualize your root chakra opening and spinning with energy.

In Spain and England, many homes don't have addresses, but names. Name your home; call it something positive, as it is your base of operations, your safety.

Adopt a tree. It doesn't have to be in your yard; it could be in front of a store or in the park. Look after its well-being; speak to it softly as you pass.

If you could be reincarnated as an animal, think about what would you choose to be and why.

What creative thing did you do as a child? Dress up? Sing or act? Play an instrument? Do it again today.

Visualization

When you create something, you do it first in your thoughts. Thinking about what you are going to make for dinner always precedes the shopping and the cooking. Thinking about something new to wear always precedes the shopping and the purchase. The idea is the blueprint for the future reality.

Focus on your physical connection to the earth. Close your eyes and visualize your feet and legs, which provide you with the locomotion to perform all the life tasks that are necessary to get sustenance from the earth and your environment, sending out roots that can travel through anything and then connect—first with the earth—and then with the rocks and minerals below.

Visualize your feet surrounded with a swirling cloud of fiery red primal energy, pumping healthy red blood up your legs to flow through your veins, giving strength to your connection to the planet, providing security to those who love and support you presently, and encouragement to those who will come to love and support you and your place on earth in the future.

See the energy of the root chakra from the earth entering your body through the soles of your feet, traveling up your legs to the base of your spine, strengthening and supporting you.

You can create a meditation that is truly unique and meaningful to you and where you are in your life at the moment. You can write your own affirmation to accompany it. As your life changes and improves, you can alter and renew your affirmation and your meditation when the need arises. Affirmations should always be framed in a positive manner. The meaning of the word is to "make firm" or positive, and stating it is a method of making it firm for yourself. Affirmations should be strong, positive statements that something is *already* in existence. By telling yourself that something actually already exists, these thoughts actually create the energy in the universe to bring what you desire into your life. If you need help to begin:

Root Chakra Meditation

"As I breathe in, I inhale the good things of life,
I exhale and leave behind me all that I no longer need or
    desire.
I am deeply connected to Mother Earth,
My life is stable and I am strong."

Root Chakra Affirmation

"I choose to create a life that is joyous and abundant."
"I choose to find a lover who is secure and balanced."

You should always end with some positive statement to yourself such as:

"This or something better now manifests for me."

Root Chakra Future

As you become more grounded, you will see that friends and lovers who are stable and reliable will come into your life. Wait with positive expectations and you will find that to be true.

The tasks may seem simple. When you have completed them, you will find that they are a starting place for you to create and invent some of your own. As you do, you will have found a release for your own original thinking and will open a well of creativity that you have held in check. Let it go, let it flow, and you will discover small tasks, tiny treats that will open a surge of power from the universe to energize and empower you.

6 Heal the Way You Give and Receive Pleasure

Love conquers all

—Virgil 37 B.C.

. . . except poverty and toothaches.

—Mae West

"He's so cute!" "He has a *great* butt!" "She's *really* hot!" "Wow, what a body!" Ah, lust, the strong emotion that even President Jimmy Carter admitted to having during the presidential campaign in 1976, when he said, "I have looked on a lot of women with lust. I've committed adultery in my heart many times. God recognizes I will do this and forgives me."

Lust is that intense, overwhelming, driving sexual craving that can consume our thoughts and our fantasies and can be described in complex clinical terms that eliminate all rational thought from the process. Can it be that lust is nothing more than the stimulation of our hormones, such as testosterone, estrogen, and pheromones, those chemicals produced by specialized glands whose sole purpose is to attract others of the same species? If it is, then when two people are attracted to each other, it doesn't seem to matter much to either of them that their horny feelings might only be biology, nothing more than human chemistry in action.

Screenwriter Nora Ephron said, "No man can be friends with a woman he finds attractive. He always wants to have sex with her. Sex is always out there. Friendship is ultimately doomed and that is the end of the story." Unfortunately, lots of people probably will agree with Nora and think that a sexual relationship is the only kind that two individuals attracted to each other can have—no friendship, no pals, no mentoring, no student–teacher relationships, no employee–employer interactions, no other types of connections and links that would allow two people to be in a relationship and be honest and open with each other, without sex being the focus.

The character Wanda the Ugly Woman on the television show *In Living Color* always said to potential lovers, "I'm gonna rock your world!" and some of us have found ourselves in a relationship that did rock our world—for a while. Others have wished to find a relationship that would be so wonderful that it would rock their world, even if it is only for a while, because almost anything is better than loneliness.

The beginning of any relationship can be ecstatic. It can cause you to lose sight of the fact that, as exciting as he is, he doesn't have a job, that she has four ex-husbands, that he asked you out and then borrowed money to pay for the evening, that she stood you up and offered a flimsy excuse for it, or any number of obvious obstacles and potentials for problems that you would point out to any friend who got involved with such a person. It is very easy to brush these problems aside as only minor, in the excitement of getting a call from this new man, touching this new woman in your life, gazing into his eyes over a candlelit dinner, allowing yourself the excitement and thrill of somebody different, who arouses you, permitting yourself to be stimulated by the fire that a new passionate experience can create.

There are lots of old proverbs that speak to the fact that love, or what we take at that moment to be love, can temporarily blind us. An old Japanese proverb says, "In the eyes of the lover, pockmarks are dimples." Comedian Lily Tomlin has been quoted as saying, "If love is the answer, could you please rephrase the question?" and another proverb cleverly points out that, "Love intoxicates you; marriage wakes you up." All of these are witty ways of restating the same thing: Infatuation, that unreasoning extravagant passion, is usually temporary. It dazzles us so that we aren't in touch with reality for the moment and sometimes so besots our brains that we behave very foolishly, often with long-term regrets. Mae West may have said it best when she pointed out that it cures everything except poverty and toothaches, because, with enough time in any relationship, those things can happen to any of us and when they do, there had better be more to the relationship than lust to see us through the difficulties.

The term *temporary infatuation* can describe almost any relationship, whether it is a friendship with another or a relationship between a boss and an employee. Until we know people long enough to understand their values and core beliefs and until we have had the opportunity to see them in times of illness, setbacks, financial troubles, employment dilemmas, and interactions with their relatives and ours, we can only view them through the superficial presentation of their "party manners" and everyday chitchat.

The Sacral Chakra

As you move upward from the grounding, or root, chakra that connects you to the earth, you become aware of the differences between yourself and others, and with that realization comes the awareness of your desires and your sexuality.

The element of water is associated with this chakra, and just as the celestial body of the moon pulls the waters of the oceans to and fro, control over the motion of all of the liquid in the universe by this chakra also includes the liquids of our bodies—such as tears, circulation, elimination, sexuality, and reproduction

The second, or sacral, chakra is located in the lower abdomen, centered between the navel and the genitals, and is considered the pleasure chakra, the one that connects to your pleasure center—it is often called the "seat of life." The sacral chakra provides the energy for pleasure, emotion, desire, and nurturance. It is where each individual expresses his or her ability to love the opposite sex, to express emotions, and to give and receive physical, mental, and spiritual pleasure. From the grounding and unity with the planet that we experience with our first or root chakra, we move now to the passions of choice, emotion, and desire that the second chakra energizes. From survival we move to the desire for pleasure, to be nurtured, and the need to reach out to others and expand our circle of those who can pleasure us in all the ways the world has to offer as well as to the expansion of our own ability to please others and enjoy life with them.

A weak sacral chakra can attract sexual predators, people who prey on the lonely, the emotionally and physically needy. An overly strong second chakra may attract those who are unwilling to make a commitment in a relationship, who may be intellectually and emotionally superficial and dependent—childish adults, who will remain in a relationship solely to have their own physical and emotional needs met.

A balanced second chakra will bring a mature, responsible, loving relationship into your life and with it the ability to find pleasure in intellectual pursuits while strengthening spiritual bonds. It is through desire that we become motivated to extend ourselves to expand and grow and so desire is a necessity. We desire nourishment, warmth, and connection to other human beings.

This chakra is a more than your sex drive. It is a palpable expression of your emotional and socializing skills. Healing this chakra will result in an aura that allows you to present yourself in both a sexually and intellectually honest manner.

Attractive People—Part A

1. Write again your list of significant others from exercise number 3. Under each name write the first thing about that person that attracted you. (Example: eyes, breasts, intelligence, talkative, good teeth, long legs, athletic, strong, funny)

   Then write how long you knew this person before the two of you became what you would consider "involved." (one week, one day, one year)

Name   _____   _____   _____
Characteristic _____   _____   _____
Time   _____   _____   _____

Never doubt that desire is a normal and beneficial emotion. Without it, you would never move forward to find satisfaction in any area of your life. However, if you find that you have focused on one particular *physical* characteristic as being an absolutely necessary factor for you to be attracted to any new possible significant other before you could consider a romantic attachment, then you might find that such a characteristic can become the equivalent of a fetish. This need to be attracted to the superficial demonstrates that your judgment and your chakra are both off-balance.

If, after being attracted to big breasts or a cute butt, you found out that this attractive person is an air-head, or too vain, or lacking in a sense of humor, or has some other character flaw, how long did it take for the relationship to end?

2. List five people you know who could potentially be dating material, but you would never consider going out with them. Add a reason for each person. (Example: too tall, flat-chested, giggles too much, bad teeth.)

   _____   _____
   _____   _____
   _____   _____
   _____   _____
   _____   _____

3. For each individual on your list, write one attribute or change they could make that would overcome your objections. (Example: wear flat shoes, see a dentist.)

   _____   _____   _____   _____

4. If they would not or could not make such a change, what would *you* be willing to change about your requirements to make dating this person possible?

   _____   _____   _____   _____

Consider that you may be restricting your opportunities to find someone wonderful by your self-limiting judgments about others.

Attractive People—Part B

1. Name someone whose physical appearance you admire. It could be anyone: a sports figure, a movie or TV star, or someone you know personally. _____

2. List five things about this person you find attractive or appealing:

_____ _____ _____ _____ _____

3. Describe behavior you admire. (For example: She tosses her hair back like a pony. He can bench press 250 pounds.)

_____

4. Select another person whose physical appearance you admire, this time someone of the opposite gender. _____

5. List five things about this person you find attractive or appealing.

_____ _____ _____ _____ _____

6. Describe behavior you admire. (Example: He has a great sense of humor. She is never loud in public.) _____

    Examine your choices. Have you: Focused on general role behaviors that are stereotyping? (Example: Females should be demure; males should be entertaining.)

    Using Items 3 and 5, reverse them. If you selected a strong male figure, when you reverse the role specific behaviors, does this change make you uncomfortable? Yes___ No___

If you have strong gender stereotypical behavioral expectations, you may severely limit your potential choices. Gender role choices may cause you to connect with individuals whose behavior may not be beneficial to you. (For example, if you believe that the man should always be in charge in a relationship, you may create a power imbalance that could be harmful.) You may need to strengthen and balance your pleasure chakra so that you create an aura that is positive and strong.

Your Persona

Your persona is your public image, the one you display to the world and that you believe may be quite different from your inner self.

1. From the following list, select the word that would best describe what you think is the first impression most people have of you:

Biker	Athlete
Computer Geek	Nerd
Babe	Socialite
Comedian	Professional
Loser	Workaholic
Sexy	Flirt
Artist	Thrill-seeker
Rocker	Intellectual
Winner	Gangster

   If none of these apply, then write down one you think does apply to you._____

2. List five reasons why you think people have this first impression:
   It doesn't take much thought to realize that first impressions are often based on (1) your physical appearance, and (2) the way you dress or your possessions, such as an expensive watch or an exotic car. However, first impressions are fleeting and although you may present yourself in a self-protecting disguise, it won't take long for others to feel your aura and become aware of the true you. (Example: "He may look like a tough biker, but he's really a big old teddy bear." "She uses big words to appear to be an intellectual, but she really doesn't know what they mean.")

   _____ _____ _____ _____ _____

3. If you don't like the first impression people have of you and you would like to change it, what would you change?

   _____ _____ _____ _____ _____

4. List specific things you would have to do to change that first impression. Now do them.

_____ _____ _____ _____ _____

Your Predominant Quality

From the following lists, circle the words that would best describe what you think is the general overall impression that most people you know have of you:

Number 1	*Number 2*
clever	silly
cool	tough
thoughtful	irresponsible
intelligent	stupid
sexy	frigid
funny	introverted
shy	perfectionist
adventurous	lazy
sympathetic	extravagant
dependable	sarcastic
sensitive	loser
honest	theatrical
serious	childish
trustworthy	careless
joyous	grouchy
fun-loving	boring

If none of these apply, then write down one you think does fit you. _____

The overall impression people have of you is usually based on their interactions with you over a period of time, as opposed to a first impression. After that first impression, people intuit your aura, the real you that you attempt to hide behind a facade. The meaning of these descriptive terms can range from one extreme of the spectrum to the other, or could be appropriate in some situations and not in others. (Example: *Intelligent* could mean you are usually bright, to appearing to be a genius. *Adventurous* could mean that you are willing to have some fun, to the extreme of taking dangerous risks.) .

Now is when you need to give thought to what you want to change and make definite plans about what you are going to do. As you progress, you will be happier with yourself and will find that you receive what you deserve. Pleasure is one of the essential features of the second chakra, which is vital for the health and balance of your body, and the elevation of your spirit. A balanced chakra will draw people to you for personal and social relationships. You will begin to move toward that which brings you pleasure and away from that which is painful.

If you have circled more words in list number 2 than in list number 1, you may want to consider trying to correct or balance some of those negative attributes. (Example: If you are theatrical in your behavior at work, where it isn't appropriate, perhaps joining an amateur theatrical group would provide an outlet for this quality. If people seem to think you are boring, you might ask others about something they are interested in and make yourself pay attention to what they have to say for five minutes.)

Larry

Larry is just a little shorter than the average guy. Not too short, but he usually felt insecure around the big guys in the gym. "I've worried about my height all my life, but I never let anyone know that I felt uncomfortable about it. I work out, keep my waist trim, stay in good shape, and I walk with a confidence I usually don't feel."

While Larry says he feels attracted to almost any woman, he admitted he prefers them big and busty, with lots of blond hair. "I know I don't think about the kind of person she might be, I just care about how she'll look to the other guys when I walk in someplace with her and then how quickly I can get her into bed—and then I'll brag about it. I'll be blunt about it. I'm not really interested in any kind of commitment because when I get tired of her, I want to be able to move on without any kind of a hassle."

Larry wouldn't circle any of the words on the list but instead wrote in *winner* and *cool* to describe himself. He admitted that he qualified for quite a few of the descriptors in list number 2 but thought that his take-charge manner made up for whatever he lacked.

"Although I'm quick to lose my temper, I can talk my way out of anything, and I don't take anything from anyone," he said emphatically. "I make a good living and I always treat my women right, take them out on the town, any place they want to go, and I buy them nice stuff."

Larry readily admitted that he saw women as sexual partners only. "They have a good time and so do I, so what's the problem?" He shrugged, "Nah, I don't want to talk to them. I'm not interested in what they think about anything. I'd rather talk to guys about sports. Women don't know much about football." Larry bets on games of any kind and he's happiest sitting in a restaurant with a bunch of his buddies, figuring out the odds on the fights, baseball, football. "I'll bet on anything but soccer," he grinned.

Larry had no interest in even hearing about chakras and auras and said he was only taking the quiz to please Karen, a statuesque blond he had met while working out at the gym. "There's nothing wrong with my sex drive. It's working great!"

Karen said, "Larry is a lot of fun, he has high energy, he's very talkative and outgoing. He has lots of pals and buddies, and he has a great sense of humor, but his attitude about sex and women stinks. Any woman who gets involved with Larry will find herself relegated to the role of housekeeper.

"Unfortunately, he has some fatal flaws that keep him from ever being a real partner in a relationship, and I am very happy that I see them before I get involved. He says he's living his life with passion, but I say he's living very superficially. While I'd like to get to know him better because he does have some charming ways, I believe he is too childish and one-dimensional. When I tried to talk to him about his pleasure chakra, he didn't want to hear anything about caring, sharing, nurturance, love thy neighbor—only about sex." Karen paused for a moment and then she said, "His second chakra is *way* out of balance."

Karen

A few months later, Karen, the statuesque blond who should have been the woman of Larry's dreams, was very excited about working with her aura.

"I thought at first that Larry had potential, but I've been through a few relationships that I believed would work if only 'I would just love him more.' I've stuck it out in unfulfilling relationships, telling myself, 'It will work, I know it can, if I just love him more. He'll make the changes I think I need him to make, if I just love him more.' Or, 'If we just love each other enough, we will be able to work these things out, no matter how big or impossible they seem.'

"I think it took meeting Larry to make me wonder how I could possibly have thought anything like that, that a guy like that was interesting for even one evening. I've watched him at the gym for quite a while now, and he goes from one new girl to another, trying to score. They all eventually give him the brush-off. Poor guy, he's actually pretty pitiful. I wonder if he'll ever wake up to how shallow his life is or just end up a lonely old man. Unfortunately, there are lots of men just like him, men who just aren't husband material. I know someone who married that kind of a man, and all she did was take care of him. She picked his clothes up off the floor, cooked his meals, kept his house clean, and waited around for him to come home. She would stay up waiting, even if he didn't come in until after midnight because he had been out with his pals. I remember her saying that she looked forward to having children because she felt that might keep her from feeling so lonely. She actually didn't expect him to change when the children arrived; she just thought it was a way for her to have something more in her life."

Karen pushed her hair back, "I used to childishly believe all the things I saw in the movies or read in romance novels. I was dedicated to the idea that 'love conquers all' and when problems arose I just kept quiet, hoping they would go away, because I didn't want to rock the boat. I have learned from sorry experience that when a guy is unable to tell me how he feels, pushes his emotions away because he thinks it isn't manly, and flirts with every waitress while I'm sitting across from him at the table, then I'd better take a good long look before I even think about getting involved. I know now that I am slowly expanding my consciousness because I have become more aware of myself as an individual who is of value, and that awareness has increased my perception of my need to connect with others on a more than one-dimensional basis. I'm thriving on the changes I'm making because it is awakening me, stimulating me to ask questions about myself, about my femininity and what I really want, what pleases me.

"I was pushing myself to have a great body, going to the gym, calorie counting to a point that was becoming obsessive. I wasn't allowing myself the simple pleasures of life, like a little extra sleep on Saturday mornings, a long walk in the woods on a sunny afternoon, or wearing comfortable clothing, because I was always worried that I wouldn't be readily available to go out if somebody called, or I that wouldn't be attractive enough to compete with younger, prettier women.

"I know that the second chakra relates to giving love, understanding, and support to others in your life and that this kind of personal growth takes time and patience. I also appreciate that to be a tender, loving, and caring human being, I must be able to nurture myself as well as others. I'm working on being more empathetic to my family, to the people I consider my friends, and as that happens I believe that someone worth caring about, someone compatible, will come into my life.

"In my visualization I'm creating a caring loving relationship for myself in the future. I believe I can make it happen."

Ask the question. Your intuition will provide the answer.

Sacral Chakra Tasks

Get a massage.

Light an orange candle and place it next to you as you bathe. Close your eyes and feel the warm water flowing over your body, cleansing and healing you. Ask the universe to help you to understand your emotions and increase your creativity in the ways that you seek and give pleasure in your relationships with all other living creatures.

How long has it been since you read some poetry? Read and memorize a short poem today.

What is the first thing you would do if your doctor told you that you had only one year to live?

Recall a dream that gave you the answer to a troubling question. Plan to dream again tonight.

Visualization

Pour a glass of clean water and sit quietly while you drink it. See that cleansing water has the ability to take away any negativity that currently exists in your life. Close your eyes and imagine that it is cleansing and healing your sacral chakra, strengthening and energizing it, bringing energy from the universe to you through to the site of your procreation, your creativity, activating your femininity or your masculinity and all that means to you. Visualize your genitals surrounded in a whirling cloud of bright orange energy, giving strength to your connection to the oceans of the world, and bringing those individuals who will enter your life to love and support you in the rivers of change that are to come.

You can create your own meditation that is based on your present needs to strengthen or unblock this chakra. As your life changes, you should rewrite and renew it so that your meditation is always a living and creative part of your life.

You must be willing to accept the best that life has to offer you because the universe is made up of pure energy, the nature of it is to constantly move and flow. The nature of life is constant change, so you must tune in to the rhythm in order to give and receive freely. Accept the goodness the universe offers so that you can share it with others. When you do this, you make space for more goodness from the universe to flow in.

Sacral Chakra Meditation

"As I breathe in, I inhale courage, pleasure, and social awareness.
As I exhale, I leave behind me vanity and worry.
The rivers of life flow through my veins to bring me joy and faith.
My life is significant and I am worthy of true love."

Sacral Chakra Affirmation

"I know that I am loved, nourished, and supported by the changing tides of the universe."
"I choose a lover to come into my life who is nurturing and strong."

Sacral Chakra Future

As you become more open to pleasure, friends and lovers who are emotionally mature will come into your life. Wait with positive expectation. They will come. Know that every moment of your life is infinitely creative and the universe is endlessly bountiful. Send forth a clear request and your heart's desire will come to you.

7 Heal Your Ability to See Yourself

What lies behind us and what lies before us are
small matters compared to what lies within us.

—Ralph Waldo Emerson

When you think about finding balance in your lives, you are probably thinking about the juggling act of home, family, and work. If you talk about balance in reference to your body, you usually think about being able to stand upright, to walk without stumbling, and maybe to dance a little without appearing to be a total klutz. The solar plexus chakra provides balancing energy to create action and power, to have a sense of self, to make choices.

The Center of Your Being

In Asian philosophies the center of one's being is located, not in the heart or in the head, but at the solar plexus, the site of the third chakra. In China today many martial arts performers earn their living performing spectacular feats in public. They perform exploits that seem impossible, such as having another person break a stack of bricks balanced on top of their heads with a sledge hammer, balancing their bodies on a sharp steel spear, splitting a thick board with their hands or downing a much larger opponent with little apparent effort. These individuals have learned to direct their attention and their energy, not to the act they are about to perform, but to their solar plexus as the focus for generating the energy needed to perform what may appear to the uninitiated as a spectacular act of strength, balance, and skill. While we struggle to balance all that we must do in our lives, while we feel over-whelmed, overworked, and constantly under stress, these artists seem very much in control, serene, healthy, and in harmony with the world.

It is almost impossible to pick up a magazine or turn on the television without reading or seeing something about the benefits of exercise and controlling your diet. Even performing a small amount of exercise, such as a walk in the evening after dinner, can make you feel good, perform better, experience higher levels of en-ergy and stamina, and keep your weight stabilized. Everyone has heard so much about limiting the fat in the diet that you become paranoid while grocery shopping, as you try to decipher the labels on all those packages, looking for fat grams and calories. While it is easy to be aware that you need to exercise and control your diet, it is not so easy to convince yourself that you need to get out and jog until you break a sweat, strain your muscles with heavy weights, and limit your intake of the foods you enjoy to reach some idealized weight or body image that magazines and television have set for us.

It is even more difficult to convince yourself that perhaps you ought to forget the laundry, forget finishing that report you've been avoiding, forget taking the time to balance the checkbook and look over the kids' homework, and that what you should do is read a book, spend the afternoon visiting a friend, go to the movies, or lie on your back watching the clouds drift by. When you become focused on one area of your life, on your responsibilities, or on a special interest to the exclusion of all others, you not only appear obsessive and behave obsessively, you find that ultimately your life is out of kilter, your health is poor, relationships with family, friends, and life partners suffer and your temper is far too short. It doesn't take long for such a frazzled life to begin to show, as other people become aware that you need a vacation, you need a few laughs, seem to have lost your sense of humor, haven't taken care of your health, and need to enjoy your life more. Sometimes it is very obvious that you are in emotional, physical, and spiritual trouble, in some instances coming apart at the seams—because it all shows up in a warped and distorted aura, which is soon apparent to anyone who comes into contact with you.

In order to have an aura that projects the image of a balanced, healthy and dynamic individual, it is important that you harmoniously integrate your body with the universe. It is very easy in your busy life to forget that there is both an art and a science for protecting and strengthening your health, prolonging your life, and living in a manner that is balanced and sensible.

Expand Your Horizons

Qi, in traditional Chinese medicine, is the term used to describe the vital breath, life force, or energy. This concept has no direct counterpart in Western culture, but it is roughly the equivalent of "bio-energy" or electromagnetic energy. This living energy is the vital life that permeates all of nature. In China more than 70 million people come together in parks every morning to do a series of slow, graceful exercises known as Tai Chi, which increase their energy levels and build stamina and flexibility, as well as reduce stress. These Tai Chi poses encourage the body to return to the pliability of childhood as the practitioner moves his or her entire physical being as one unit.

A classic Hindu philosophy uses one of its systems, a method of developing the physical body through symmetry, flexibility, and strength, known as Hatha Yoga and is offered at health centers in almost every city in Western society. One posture, known as the Sun Pose, is performed by most devotees upon arising and in recognition of the renewed energy given to everyone by the reappearance of the sun each morning. In this exercise a series of stretches takes the body slowly through a flexing of each and every muscle, accompanied by controlled breathing. One of the beautiful things that happens when someone practices Tai Chi or Yoga, or another of the stretching and flexibility exercise routines, is that they stretch and expand more than their muscles and tendons.

They also stretch their consciousness, expand their horizons, and beautify and amplify their aura.

Many people have lost the innate capacity to move naturally, as animals do. Their movements are controlled instead by human emotional states, sudden thoughts and reactions that have built up over decades of misuse. The result are damaged joints, sore muscles, and rigidity of thought that can lead to anxiety, depression, and ultimately serious illness.

For thousands of years practitioners of these various doctrines have recognized that they are more than exercises. They are a self-conscious effort at achieving harmony between the individual and the cosmos. People have come to realize that without flexibility of the body, rigidity of thinking is inevitable.

Living Creatures

There are other ways to rebalance our chakras: for example, when we give time to other living things in the universe—plants and animals. Studies over the last decade have shown that pet ownership appears to enhance your health and well-being because pets can provide richness and texture to your life.

In one study at the University of Australia it was found that pet owners had lower cholesterol, trigliceride, and blood pressure levels and those who had had a heart attack were nine times more likely to live one year longer than non-pet owners. The natural emotional outlet pets provide can create a therapeutic relaxation response. The medical community knows that the damaging effects of loneliness and depression can be offset by the simple act of caring for something other than yourself because it helps you to remember that you are a part of a greater whole.

Knowing Who You Are

The third or solar plexus chakra is the location of personal and of your intention concerning your physical health, as of knowing "who you are." It is the physical location where you experience many emotions. It is where we feel queasy when we are nervous and where we should locate our power when we want to feel strong and sure of ourselves. The term *solar plexus* implies a connection to the sun, with a fiery energy that brings us warmth and power—our will and vitality. With fire as its element, it is responsible for the regulation and distribution of energy throughout the body.

We have moved from the survival energy of the first or root chakra, through the passions of desire and pleasure that are energized by the second or sacral chakra, to the third chakra, which energizes a balanced life and brings the transformation of this energy into action and power. At the solar plexus you can reach deep into your sense of self and find a point of balance between the extremes of your desires and passions by understanding and transforming them, using your passion and desire to direct your actions.

A weak third chakra allows you to be afraid or feel powerless, lonely, and depressed, and when that happens, you may withdraw, narrowing the field of your chakra so that it hardly extends more than an inch from your body, causing you to appear cold and controlled. A weak third chakra attracts illness, as well as those who prey on people who are physically fragile, low in energy, and lacking a strong will. A strong third chakra brings those who admire others with physical and mental energy while it repels other people whose interests are limiting and shallow.

Chakra to Chakra

The chakras are interdependent. They do not act separately, and only in our thinking do we separate them because it makes it easier for us to understand their functions. However, we build on the lower chakras to provide a balanced interaction with the physical world and we will continue to build on the upper chakras to provide stability for them so that the spirituality and intuition that the higher chakras provide can course easily in and out and create a powerful total energy flow from the universe, which actuates our aura.

Power Point of View

Circle each item that you feel applies to you:

1. It's not my fault.
2. I am just a victim of circumstances.
3. I always have bad luck.
4. If I just wait, something is bound to change.
5. I am waiting for good things to happen.
6. I hope that this pain will go away.
7. The world isn't fair.
8. I'll never do that again.
9. Everyone probably feels sorry for me.
10. When I win the lottery, things will be different.
11. I was just in the wrong place at the wrong time.

If you circled even one of the items on this list, you chose an expression of "poor me," a very negative emotional position, but one that is easy to take. While it will take some effort, particularly when things are going badly and you feel abused by the whole world, you must make an attempt to raise yourself above this feeling of powerlessness. If you feel that somehow the world has conspired to bring you whatever unfortunate circumstances, whatever harsh and painful life lessons you are experiencing, you are not taking responsibility for your own life. Whatever the circumstances in which you find yourself, no matter how unpleasant and unhappy the life events you have experienced, the truth is that, unfortunately, life events happen to us all.

When you take responsibility for whatever has happened to you in your life, such as unsatisfactory careers and rotten relationships, you begin to take control. By taking responsibility you recognize that the choices were yours, you made them, and now you have the power to alter them from this point forward. Once you take control, once you take your power back, you are no longer a victim of circumstances. That positive power thinking will immediately affect your chakras and alter your aura.

It is very easy to look at someone else's life and think that person never had the disappointment or the trauma that has befallen you. Since none of us can be inside another person's life, you cannot really know how someone else feels. You must now accept that you recognize the yang and yin of creation, the duality of the world. As it is described in Asian philosophies, this duality as it applies to each individual is explained by simple statements such as: Without darkness, you would not understand or appreciate the light; without rain, you would not understand or appreciate the sunshine; without pain and sorrow, you cannot appreciate or understand joy and pleasure. You must recognize that as terrible as your present difficulty may be, nothing is forever.

You must not deny your past. Instead, you must incorporate that past into the experience and knowledge that will create opportunities for you to take new and action-oriented choices.

Rewrite *all* of the previous items into positive power point of view affirmations, whether you think they apply to you or not. Doing so will create positive reinforcement in your consciousness. (Example: While it was not my fault, I will use what I learned to make better choices. Luck has nothing to do with it, I will now move in a new direction.)

Who Are You?

Make a list of ten descriptors you might use if asked to tell someone who you are. (Example: Wife, father, lawyer, theologian, student, housewife, lover, comedian, realtor, singer, coach, nurse, swimmer, artist, poet.) Go back over your list and add a percentage of the time in the last week you spent actively being that person. (Example: It is very easy to figure out how much time you spent on your income-producing occupation, and, of course, you are a wife or a father 100 percent of the time, but how much of your day did you *actively* devote to being that wife or that father?)

_____   _____   _____   _____   _____

_____   _____   _____   _____   _____

Creating Balance Creates Joy

Make a list of ten things you enjoy doing that have nothing to do with work, chores, or other obligations: (Even if you really like ironing or cleaning your golf clubs, do not include them.) (Example: Soaking in the tub, reading for pleasure, roller blading, making love, hiking, painting, attending church, visiting a museum, playing the piano, photographing nature.) Go back over your list and write down the last time you did each of these joy-creating activities.

_____   _____   _____   _____   _____

_____   _____   _____   _____   _____

Go back over your list again and write down the last time you did any of these activities with someone else.

As you look over these exercises, you will probably find that some balance is missing. Perhaps you are a workaholic or your focus is on keeping your house clean, and the things you think of as fun you haven't done for months.

Go back to your Who Are You? exercise and write beside it the kind of person who might be attracted to the individual you described. If 50 percent of your time is spent at your job, who might that be? Do not answer with who you might meet at work but whom you might attract by being absorbed in your work. Another workaholic? A person interested in how much money you can earn quickly? If you spend most of your time cleaning, would a neat freak attract slobs, looking for someone to pick up after them all the time? If you enjoy photographing nature and think that another nature photographer might be just the right person for you, but you only spend 1 percent of your time doing that and haven't done it for months, perhaps you need some serious rebalancing of how you spend your time. If Mr. or Ms. Right is a nature photographer, you aren't going to meet that person while you are out in the garage working on your car or doing another load of laundry.

As you look at how you spend your time, divide your life into the following eight activities. Play might include exercise and friends, and food might include shopping and cooking, work could include both at home and at your job, but however you divided it up, rewrite it, dividing it into the kind of balance you would *truly* like these things to have in your life.

Activities	Percent of Your Life	Percent of Your Rebalanced Life
Work		
Play		
Exercise		
Food		
Learning		
Friends		
Romance		
Spirituality		

The balance you select is yours alone. If you really like working and that is how you want to spend a large percentage of your life, it is your choice. If you see that your life is out of balance, rearrange it as you would wish it to be for you to be happy. As you compare your rebalanced life to your current schedule, list one thing that you can do immediately to shift this balance. (Example: Learning: Buy a book on a topic you have wanted to know more about. Friends: Call up a friend and make a plan to meet for coffee. Spirituality: Look for a meditation class. Play: Stop by a garage sale and add to your coffee mug collection or try a new recipe.)

One-Day Food Diary

Make a list of everything you ate *yesterday* and don't forget the doughnut with your morning coffee and the buttered popcorn last night while you watched TV. Do not select a more perfect day, one that you would feel a lot better about seeing on the page, because you are making an attempt to honestly evaluate your eating habits. We all know that unless we feel well, we don't function efficiently in any area of our lives. It is very easy to fall into unhealthy eating habits, particularly if we feel lonely or emotionally deprived.

Morning   Noon   Evening

Look over your list; perhaps you could improve your dietary habits. Most of us could. Plan to make one small change. (Example: Use one teaspoon of salad dressing instead of two. Buy some apples for that late-night snack.) Add to this section, how many times you exercised this week.

Now write an affirmation about it: (Example: Starting today I will _____.)

Affirm: _____.

If you have avoided exercising or have put it low on your list of priorities, see if you could divide it up into smaller increments during the day. (Example: A brief walk in the morning, another short one at noon, or perhaps you could take the stairs instead of the elevator, or park at the outer edge of the lot when you stop to buy groceries.)

List some creative ways you could improve your ability to get exercise into your day.

_____

_____

_____

_____

Now write an affirmation about it. (Example: Starting today I will _____.)

Affirm: _____.

Connect With Your New Power

Circle on this list the positive things you have made happen in your lifetime with your power:

Add some of your own to the list.

1. A home
2. A car
3. A wardrobe
4. An organization you contributed something to
5. Poetry you wrote
6. The birthday party you gave for a friend
7. The bike you repaired
8. The friends you introduced to each other
9. _____
10. _____

As you look over the list, you will see that you have done a lot of good, much of it without thought of a reward, because you do have the power to create action—an act of will, one of the governing attributes of the third chakra.

Stimulate Your Third-Chakra Power

"Knowledge is power" is a well-known expression because remaining powerless is often the result of not knowing just what to do, how to behave differently in some particular situation.

List three small changes you plan to make to increase your balance and by so doing increase your personal power.

(Example: I will set aside time to give myself a manicure. I will write in my journal.)

1. _____
2. _____
3. _____

Collect some of nature's treasures: small stones, a shell, a pretty leaf. Use them as devotional or meditation aids. As you repeat your affirmations, dedicate whatever you have collected to your specific intention to rebalance your life and thus reinforce your third-chakra power.

Create a small personal alter and place these treasures on it to remind you of your commitment to your affirmations.

Lila

Lila, a very pretty, very thin woman, had stayed in a bad relationship for years, always wanting to leave and feeling unable to do so because she felt that there was no place else for her to go.

"My parents were divorced when I was about ten. My early years seemed to be filled with the sounds of them fighting and arguing. I don't seem to remember that there was ever any fun in our house.

"When my mother remarried, I thought I might have a life like some of the other kids I knew, but I got a stepfather who was cold and distant, who never showed me any affection or praised me for anything at all. I worked hard at school and got good grades, but that was taken for granted. I was expected to stay out of trouble, help with the housework, and just stay out of their way. When my mother died of breast cancer, I was left with a stepfather who really didn't want me."

Lila smiled and looked down at her hands. "I met Todd at my first job after high school. He worked for our neighbor's lawn service and he seemed like a dream come true. Whenever I saw him, he was working quietly away with the shrubs, down on his knees spreading mulch, or running the edger around the grass with earphones on, listening to music. I took it for granted that someone who worked outside, cared for plants and living things, would be gentle, serene, and kind. I thought he seemed so patient and easy going. It never occurred to me that he was doing yard work because he didn't have a high school diploma, couldn't hold another job because he couldn't get along with any of his coworkers, or that he hated what he was doing. I guess I just jumped into a relationship with him because it was an easy out from my stepfather's house and I thought I'd be safe and protected.

"I believed that he was so different from both my real father and my stepfather, but as I look back on it now, I see that they were all very similar. Todd had a drinking problem, just like my father, and although I didn't know about it at first, I looked upon it as a challenge. I thought I could help him overcome it. I didn't see it as any kind of a medical problem; I thought it was an emotional one and with enough love from me, he wouldn't want to drink anymore. How wrong I was."

Lila smiled and twisted her hands together in her lap. "It didn't take me long to find out that Todd could fly off the handle at almost nothing at all and what did I do? I was so afraid of conflict that I just escaped into doing some housework while I tried to stay out of his way.

"When I did the Power Point of View exercise, I circled every one of those answers. I began to realize that I had to do something about allowing myself to continue to be a victim of circumstances, that I was sending out a message or an aura that said it was okay for everybody to walk all over me. I had made myself a doormat for men who liked nothing better than to have something or someone to wipe their feet on. I know now that I was seriously lacking in self-esteem, and that it is common for women who are victims of abusive partners to have a self-esteem problem.

"When I began taking the Tai Chi classes, Todd thought it was silly and he made a lot of fun of me, but as I began to think about centering my power and then began actually getting some power and strength for myself, he was no longer amused. It just made him angrier about everything. It would have been a whole lot easier to just give it up, to quit and keep him happy. But I kept thinking about my answers to the Power Point of View exercise and I knew I couldn't quit or I'd be lost, I'd be worse off than before I started. Before Tai Chi I would have thrown my hands up and resigned myself to this life. Todd just stayed angry all the time now and at the end of his day he would come in with a six-pack, flop down on the couch without a word, and drink them all.

"Meditation has really helped me. Not only to deal with the fact that I couldn't do anything about Todd's choice of reaction to what I was doing, but it also helped me see that I had to continue to work on myself and on the message I was sending to the world. I've learned a lot about organizations that help women like me, but until I had more going for me I doubt that I would even have had the courage to call one of them.

"It has taken me quite a while to connect with my power, to discover that I had actually contributed to the lives of a lot of people. I hadn't realized how much I had helped my mother when she was sick, how I actually have some skill when it comes to helping people. When I finally left Todd, I was able to do it because I realized it would be better for both of us, that I couldn't keep on saving him and still take care of myself. While we have remained friends, I know that I need to keep my balancing chakra strong and solid or I could fall right back into such a negative relationship again. Just recently I got a scholarship to go to nursing school. How is that for progress?

"A few weeks ago I was sitting on the edge of the sand at the beach, with warm water lapping at my toes. I felt the soft night wind ruffle my hair and I lifted my head up and looked at the starry sky and gazed in awe at the pale moon near the edge of the water. I knew, at that moment, that the sand, the ocean, the breeze, the stars in the sky, and that pale slice of moon were all mine. Suddenly, I felt very contented because I now realized that I was finally in the place I was meant to be. I have a lot of work to do and I know it. I'll be starting nursing school in the fall and I'm really looking forward to it. It will open a whole new world to me, a future, a career, and then, who knows what will be next. I realize I could never have done it if I hadn't had the realization from the Power Point of View that I was just sitting around feeling helpless and sorry for myself and I had to take control of my own life. I think I've finally done that.

"I've got my balancing chakra operating now and I'm feeling pretty frisky. Just watch me!"

Morris

Morris is a tall, balding man in his mid-forties. He says, "I'm a used car salesman. I've never done anything else. I've been a used car salesman since I began buying and trading cars in high school. Before I graduated, I had a regular little business going from my parent's driveway and my whole family thought I was a financial genius. By the time I was twenty-nine, I was very successful financially. I ran a little 'buy-here, pay-here' outdoor lot. I slept on a cot in a shed at the back. Night and day I'd be there, and if I heard anybody walking around, even if it was the middle of the night, I'd jump up and sell them a car.

"I helped a lot of people with bad credit. When nobody else would sell them a car, I would. I made it possible for them to have transportation so they could get to their jobs. Those folks never let me down, they were so grateful. On their day off they would show up, I'd cash their paycheck and slowly, very slowly, they would pay off those cars."

He shrugged. "I worked twenty-four hours a day, seven days a week. The ladies all love me now. They see my energy, my enthusiasm, and they see me as a good catch, a wealthy man. Everybody knows me. It doesn't matter where I go, people come up to me, remind me of the car I sold them and I always take time to speak with them because I know this is an opportunity to sell them their next car.

"At least, that was what I thought until I had my major heart attack. My mother read me these questions and wrote down my answers while I was still in the hospital with tubes running up my nose and into both arms. She had a captive audience. I wasn't really interested, but she had me trapped there in my hospital room."

Morris began pacing, raising his voice, "I have had to take advantage of every opportunity. There are lots of car dealers out there, lots of competition. Sure, I'd like to get married and have a family, but I've always put financial goals first. I felt I needed to get really established before I thought of about any of those things that my family seems to think are important.

"To say the quiz was a revelation is putting it mildly. I was very proud of what I was doing. I thought I was getting ahead in the world. It wasn't until this happened that I realized just how terrible my life was, really out of kilter. I'm well aware that I worked hard. Selling cars has been my family, my wife, my lover, my food and drink, my entertainment, my exercise. Until I got sick, it wasn't possible for me to even think about having a relationship. I'm not romantic, I'm not educated. I usually fall asleep in front of TV right after dinner because I'm exhausted. The only thing I know anything about is cars. I don't read and I haven't been to the movies or taken a vacation in years."

Morris seemed a little grim. "I've had to do a lot of reevaluating and my doctor says I have to do it quickly or I'm not going to be around to enjoy the fruits of all my hard work. My mother brought me a plant." He laughed. "She said it was a start on the road to caring about something besides cars. I just hope I don't forget to water it. The first thing I'm going to do for myself is get a dog. I had one as a child and he was a lot of fun. A dog will bark, remind me that it needs to be fed, walked."

Morris waved his hands above his head, "I sure hope I remember. A dog and a plant—that's a lot of personal responsibility for a guy like me. Meditation? I don't know about that, but this affirmation thing I believe I can do because I've always been a goal setter. I realize now that I have to make my goals about people and having a life, not about money and deals. I guess I sort of lost the humanity I had when I was helping the little guy get a car and take care of his family. I hope I can bring that back because I do remember how good it made me feel. Anyway, I'm definitely going to try."

Solar Plexus Chakra Tasks

Get a yellow T-shirt. Wear it while you do sit-ups or crunches
   to strengthen your abdominal muscles.
Treat yourself to dinner in a fancy restaurant and eat in an
   unhurried way so that you enjoy and savor the experience.
   Say your own version of Grace silently before you begin, and

stop eating as soon as you are full, even if there is still food
on your plate.

Give a small party and invite at least one person from a
generation different than your own.

Give someone a sincere compliment.

Skip the usual "Have a good day" to the clerk in the
supermarket. Try, "Stay healthy," and enjoy their surprised
response.

Smile at a stranger.

Think about a waterfall with a rainbow over it.

Visualization

Visualize the yellow glow of sunshine strengthening your own
internal authority over your future. As the sunshine warms your
solar plexus, the center of your energetic self, feel the power of
your determination to rebalance your life and focus your energy on
a joyous future. See yourself holding out your arms in greeting to
new friends. Smile as you know you will soon find pleasurable relationships in friendships and love. With your eyes closed and the
image of your strong and balanced third chakra whirling with
strength and power, bring energy into your body and send it up
and down your spine. Believe that you can rebalance your life. Ask
to discover who you really are because you *know* you are more
than the person who invests your energy in jobs, mortgages, parents, husbands, children, and lovers.

Reflect on the balance your life has and the changes you want
to make. Close your eyes and see your abdominal muscles strong
and supporting, controlling the energy and power of your physical presence.

Meditation and Affirmation

Your thoughts and your meditation will change as you change.
Rewrite your meditation and create an affirmation that is appropriate to where you are at the present moment. Meditate to discover

that you can connect with the power of the universe and through it expand and heal your aura. Meditation = reaffirmation. Repetition brings joy.

Solar Plexus Chakra Meditation

"As I breathe in, I inhale the strength and health that is mine by divine right,
As I exhale, I leave behind illness and unhealthy relationships that no longer benefit me.
I am transformed by the heat of sun.
My life is in balance and I am powerful."

Affirmation

"I choose to receive what I know I deserve."
"I choose to find a lover who is brimming with vitality and health."

Solar Plexus Future

As you become more centered, you will begin to see that friends and lovers who have a positive sense of self will come into your life. Wait with creative energy. They will arrive when you least expect them.

$\mathcal{8}$ Heal Your Openness to Life and Love

Love is a fruit in season at all times,
and within reach of every hand.

—Mother Teresa

When you think of having a loving relationship that fulfills your need for a connection to another human being, someone who will complete you, make you feel whole, it is easy to overlook all the aspects of your own and the lives of others that illustrate wholeness. You are able to be complete, whole, and without another person, although a loving other in your life would be pleasant. You have a core, a center, that can be complete by unity with an ideal, an art, a concept, a community, an idea—something that you can care about more than yourself. The heart chakra provides the energy for love and unity with others.

Heart Words

We have all been in a house in which there are no plants, no pets, no books, no art, and no music; although the people who live there have a roof over their heads, a place to sleep and prepare meals, it is not really a home in the true sense of the word.

Among the many expressions that are familiar to us are "it tugs on my heart strings," "it warms the cockles of my heart," and "she lives in my heart of hearts." Emotional expressions about someone you really love can include "he's locked into my heart," "I love him with all my heart," or "Our two hearts beat as one." Our language is filled with heart words, such as warm-hearted, meaning someone who is sympathetic and generous; big-hearted, generous and kind; soft-hearted, compassionate and tender; and there is, of course, the expression "sick-at-heart," when we are most unhappy and melancholy; or "brokenhearted," when love is rejected or finished or lost. We never make such statements about casual relationships, trips to Disneyland, short-lived affairs, meals in fancy restaurants, or one-night stands. Only when we need to convey the depth of feeling that occurs when someone or some experience has touched us at the innermost center of our being, do we speak of our core of our emotions—our heart.

The more open you are to all the experiences that life can offer, the greater your capacity is to love an evergrowing circle of life. Your heart chakra is the center through which you love yourself, your children, your family, and your significant others; your community, your state, your nation, your world, your planet. The more this heart center is open and functioning, the further this love of humanity extends, reaching the outer limits of altruism, grace, and benevolence that makes it possible for it to extend to friends, neighbors, and nations, as well as to all our fellow creatures.

The Integration Chakra

The heart chakra has another function. This is the chakra that integrates those worldly chakras below it and the chakras of your mental realms that lie above it. When the heart chakra functions at a level that is concerned with more than your individual desires and actions, it brings about an integration of mind and body, spirit and matter, and gives you a luminous sense of completeness. The element connected with this chakra is air. It brings with it loving winds and currents from throughout all of the universe, which can allow you to feel loving toward all of humanity. Accept your place in the order of things because doing so creates harmony within your soul.

When your life is in disarray, it is easy to withdraw. You should limit your contacts with the outside world in order to lessen the pain you might experience. It is easy to make the excuse that you are too busy, too stressed, or too tired to do anything more than take care of the day-to-day things your life requires. When your life is out of kilter, the easiest thing to do as a form of self-preservation, or so you often seem to think, is to disconnect not only from your loved ones but from yourself. When relationships with husbands, wives, or lovers seem to be the cause of all your heartache, and you have been disappointed over and over again, it is easy to lose yourself in work, routine, and responsibilities, to narrow your world to keep out the pain. When you stay up late doing the chores, when you work hard to buy things that you are too tired to enjoy, when you can't find time for friends, then those spontaneous moments that happen occasionally when you feel alive and well, grateful for all the good things that are in your life, don't seem to happen anymore.

When you experience that bunker mentality, keeping your head down so the world won't take another pot shot at you, then you know that not only is your heart chakra out of kilter or blocked, but you aren't going to feel authentic and engaged until you do something about it. Exhausted and overwhelmed, disappointed in the potential lovers you either meet and discard or don't have time to find, words like *peace* and *justice* are just remote terms that someone like a Mother Teresa probably thinks about and understands, but definitely not you.

The Heart Chakra

The fourth chakra, located at the center of the heart, is considered the location of love, compassion, and altruism. A weak heart chakra limits the capacity for loving others and attracts those who prey on people with good and generous hearts. A strong heart chakra allows you to affirm a love for humanity and create a balance in the ability to care about other living creatures, makes generosity possible, and increases the ability to accept an ever-increasing circle of loving people. As the heart chakra strengthens you will see the limitless possibilities of widening friendships, you will be better able to evaluate the behavior of others, and you will find more compassion in your heart for other humans, as you become more open to life and are more willing to find and accept joyous experiences.

Heal Your Openness to Life

1. Create a fantasy lover in your mind. No one will ever see this person, so you can create someone of any race, age, religion, and appearance, with any personality traits you desire. Create your perfect someone. Begin by listing their visible attributes. If something really wouldn't matter, say so.
   Height: _____ Weight: _____ Hair color: _____
   Eye Color _____ Age _____ Race _____
   Most important physical attribute _____ (Example: large breasts, perfect teeth.)

2. List the image you feel it is necessary for this fantasy lover to have:
   Religion _____ Education _____ Profession/Occupation _____
   Type of car _____ Type of Home _____ Hobby _____
   Special interests _____ (Example: football fan, avid reader.)
   Make the mental picture of your perfect someone as complete as possible. Include as much detail as you can to make this person more than a shadowy figure in your mind.

3. List your own visible attributes
   Height: _____ Weight: _____ Hair color: _____
   Eye Color _____ Age _____ Race _____
   Most visible physical attribute _____

4. List your own image attributes
   Religion _____ Education _____ Profession/Occupation _____
   Type of car _____ Type of Home _____ Hobby _____
   Special interests _____

5. Make a comparison between the two lists.

    If you are a man, did you specify a fantasy lover who would be shorter than you? Yes __ No __

    Younger than you? Yes __ No __

    If you are a woman, did you specify a fantasy lover who would be taller than you? Yes __ No __

    Older than you? Yes __ No __

    If you selected a person of a culture other than your own, list three people of that cultural origin you known personally. (Do not include celebrities.)

_____ _____ _____

    List one trait or attribute for each of these people that you admire.

_____ _____ _____

    List one cultural difference that you can foresee that might create a problem in a relationship. (Example: Certain cultures frown on public displays of affection, even hand holding.)

_____

    If you selected a person of a different faith from your own, list three people of that religion you know personally. (Do not include celebrities.)

_____ _____ _____

    List one ethical attribute for each of these people that you appreciate.

_____ _____ _____

    List one religious difference you can foresee that might create a problem in a relationship. (Example: Honoring a different day of the week as the Sabbath.) _____

    If your dream mate should have an educational level different from your own, write two reasons why.

_____ _____

    List five reasons for the choice of profession/occupation you want your fantasy lover to have.

_____ _____ _____ _____ _____

List five personality traits you want this lover to possess.

_____ _____ _____ _____ _____

A couple may be able to overlook a large age difference in the beginning of the relationship, but as time goes by the fact that one member wants to stay out late on a Saturday night while the other is tired or just wants to stay home can become a problem that will only become larger with time. Older partners can get tired of explaining about something that happened before the younger partner was born, and the younger ones can certainly get tired of hearing about something that has no significance to them, such as the Vietnam war, a bad hip, or diet restrictions. The older person may become impatient by immature behavior or lack of experiences that both of them can relate to, and can easily begin to act like a parent rather than a partner. The younger partner might begin to resent having to defer to the wisdom of the older mate and may find that friends, activities, and interests seem childish to their mate; they may begin to let the older partner fill the disciplinary parental role, to the dissatisfaction of both.

Religious differences are seldom a problem in the beginning of a relationship, but when the holidays arrive, some of the issues that were never discussed or were not a problem before can become important issues. Which set of parents to visit, what holiday customs to observe, or explaining customs that seem downright weird can often precipitate difficulties.

The issue of children and the religion in which they are raised can often become a problem that is almost too difficult to overcome, even with couples who, although they enjoy the customs and the rituals of their respective religions, have never been too connected to their traditions before they thought of surrendering their children to another religion. They now find many objections to raise about the religious beliefs of the other person.

Interracial couples may find that Kwanzaa or Ramadan are more than just interesting cultural events but instead create barriers that they had never even considered in the relationship.

There are no correct or incorrect answers to this exercise. They are simply part of an examination of how you see yourself in relation to others, of your understanding of your own self-worth, and of the importance you might place on physical appearance, image, careers, possessions, or religious beliefs. This exercise can be helpful in looking at how your view of physical appearance might prevent you from seeing the real person, someone who will be overlooked in your search for Mr. or Ms. Right.

There is a oft-quoted myth that "true loves conquers all." While that may be possible in some situations because people can work on their differences, certain differences might require adjustments that are not possible.

After you complete your exercise, you might decide that ethnic or cultural differences were attractive to you because they were mysterious or exotic, without actually knowing whether they would be problematic in a relationship or whether stereotyping has limited you in your choices. If that is so, then you are on the way to thinking beyond them, expanding your universe, and increasing the strength and power of your heart chakra.

Wholeness Exercise

I have at least one live plant in my home.	Yes ___	No ___
I worked outside in the yard or garden recently.	Yes ___	No ___
I have a pet.	Yes ___	No ___
I read for pleasure.	Yes ___	No ___
I listen to more than one type of music.	Yes ___	No ___
I have photographs of loved ones on display.	Yes ___	No ___
I have art (prints, paintings, drawings) on my walls.	Yes ___	No ___
I have a hobby.	Yes ___	No ___
I sometimes sing, whistle, or hum when I'm alone.	Yes ___	No ___
I participate in at least one charitable activity.	Yes ___	No ___

I belong to an organization that has nothing
   to do with my work.   Yes ___   No ___

I called a friend just to say "hello" in the past
   month.   Yes ___   No ___

I picked up a smooth stone and carried it in
   my pocket.   Yes ___   No ___

I recently went outside and looked at the
   moon.   Yes ___   No ___

I lit a scented candle when I was alone.   Yes ___   No ___

For every "no" answer you marked, you probably have an excuse. For example, "I can never keep a plant alive, I don't have a
green thumb, indoor plants are too messy, and anyway, I usually
forget to water them," or "Pets aren't allowed where I live and besides, I travel for my job and don't have anyone to take care of a
pet while I'm gone," or "I don't have time to read anything but stuff
related to my job, most novels are too long, they are just a waste
of time, and besides, I don't have a good book right now."

As you think about your excuses, you may realize that these are
not reasons, they are excuses, because you are too busy, too weepy,
too hurt, too tired. The real reason that most of us hide from ourselves and from the rest of the planet is that when our lives are
painful and burdensome, things of the heart and the spirit are difficult to do because they ask us to open up our heart chakra at a
time when it seems constricted, too heavy, and too painful to do so.

Raise Your Spirits and Lift Your Heart

Lots of excellent research exists describing the benefits of many of
these spirit-enhancing, heart-lifting activities. Scottish researchers
have found that a daily dose of Mozart significantly brightens the
moods of institutionalized stroke victims. Psychological tests showed
that patients receiving twelve weeks of daily music therapy were less
depressed and anxious, and more stable and sociable. Researchers
have known for a long time that music can directly influence

pulse, blood pressure, and the electrical activity of the muscles, and they suspect that it can actually help build and strengthen connections among nerve cells.

Zoologist James Serpell at the University of Pennsylvania reports that people with pets have fewer minor health problems, that blood pressure drops and cholesterol and triglyceride levels are markedly lower when anyone simply strokes a cat or a dog.

Dentists report that watching fish in an aquarium soothes as effectively as hypnosis, and other scientists report that our instinctive bond to animals is so great that humans find psychological comfort in being with any animal, even a turtle. UCLA psychologist Judith Siegel reported that a pet provides something to focus on, a sense of attachment and of being valued unconditionally. After studying the impact animals have on producing significantly better emotional well-being, Dr. Karen Allen, a research scientist at the State University of New York at Buffalo, said, "If this were a drug and you showed such significant improvement, it would be considered effective."

Get Involved

Researchers at Cornell University have demonstrated that when you help others, you help yourself and that members of volunteer organizations live longer. Bestselling author Dr. Dean Ornish has found that people who are socially involved are two to five times less likely to suffer from heart disease. Allan Luks, in his book *The Healing Power of Doing Good,* writes that volunteers experience a "helper's high" as well as an elevated sense of well-being. Luks says that the most successful volunteer efforts involve personal contact, regular participation, and an activity that matches your skills and interests.

Wholeness Tasks

Buy a small, inexpensive plant. (It could be a cactus or
  something equally hardy.)

Do one small thing in the yard or outside, even picking up a
   piece of trash.

Consider a pet. (A fish or a turtle are allowed in apartments.)

Think of whom you would ask to take care of it when you are
   away. (Remember, it could go to that friend's place.)

Begin a book you chose for pleasure.

For a few minutes tune your radio to an unfamiliar music
   station.

Pull out an old photo and put it up somewhere. (It doesn't
   need a frame to go on the refrigerator.)

Put a piece of art on your wall. (It could be a birthday card or a
   child's drawing.)

Consider a hobby you always thought you would like to do.

Whistle, sing, or hum as you comb your hair.

Do something for someone else. (Writing a check doesn't
   count.)

Join an organization. (Look in the yellow pages or on the
   Internet for some ideas.)

Phone a friend you haven't called for a while.

Pick up a stone and carry it with you. (You might even rub
   your fingers over it once in a while.)

Go outside and look at the moon for several minutes.

Light a scented candle.

Remember to choose to be happy.

Add to this list ten things you could do that would heighten
your sensitivity to the world around you, things that you can do
easily that will nourish your heart. (Example: visit a greenhouse,
dance, walk in the rain, attend church, browse a bookstore on your
lunch hour, pet a dog, go hiking, take a class, write a song.) You
will discover that some simple pleasure, such as reading a new
book or listening to enjoyable music for a few minutes, can make
you feel good because doing so diverts your mind for a few moments from the pressing issues of your life.

   As you do these things, you will see that some of them are more
painful than others, perhaps because they remind you of a happier

time or an enjoyable experience with someone you were in love with. If so, you may find that you are you are more resistant to doing them, even though they might be simple, such as looking at the moon or picking up a book to read. Use this as a clue to think about why that may be—perhaps because the activity is memory-provoking or a reminder of mistakes you think you may have made in the past. Mistakes are only mistakes if you don't use them to learn. The heartbreaks of the past can easily make anyone cynical, and you should make a definite choice that you won't allow that to happen.

Decide to opt for the promise and magic of your life's future and let the past go.

Visualization Skills

Your life can change; your ability to attract the kind of lover or friend who will treat you with compassion, kindness, love, and trust can grow. One of the skills that will help you change your aura and turn your dreams into reality is to visualize exactly what you want. Many doctors and psychotherapists now use a technique known as "visual imagery," or to be more precise, "waking dream" therapy, to treat their patients with both physical and emotional problems. Today, pain clinics and cancer centers throughout the United States find that utilizing what they call the bodymind unity has brought people relief from pain when nothing else would and relief from their disease when nothing else could.

Multimillionaires and Olympic athletes, motivational trainers and top salespeople, Ted Turner and Henry Ford, and Venus Williams, Richard Simmons and Deepak Chopra, Zig Ziglar and Robert Schuller, Anthony Robbins and Robert Weill all say that they use visualization regularly in their lives. Visualization is about possibilities and desired futures. A vision of the future can be an expression of optimism and hope because a mode of thinking based on visions opens you to considered possibilities, not simply probabilities. To envision your future as positive, filled with love and purpose, you must be able to draw upon that very natural mental process of creating images. When you invent a future for yourself, you need to create a mental picture of what things will be like long before you begin that journey.

Images are your windows on the world of tomorrow. When you talk about going places you've never been, with a wonderful life companion at your side—whether to the top of an unclimbed mountain or to the pinnacle of success in an entirely new career—you must imagine what this journey and this companion will look and be like. These visions, these dreams for the future, become real when you make them into concrete terms. Just as architects make drawings and engineers build models, you must visualize to give expression to your hope for the future. You can use this potent power to create pictures of all the good you would like to see enter your life.

Determine what you want. If you want a man who is tall, dark, and handsome, one who is compassionate, sensual, loving, and brave—say so. If you want a woman who is petite, blond, and beautiful, one who is charming, calm, and romantic—say so. If you have a burning passion, a dream, a personal agenda that must be met, you must visualize it and him or her. You must *want* such a romantic encounter, one that will result in a significant relationship, to happen.

Try the following experiment:

Close your eyes, take a few deep breaths:

Think about Paris. Even if you have never been there, you have seen enough movies, looked at enough photographs, to have an idea of what it must be like. Think of the Eiffel Tower, the Arc de Triomphe, the Seine, Notre Dame, good food, wine, romance; the music that helps create these images can play in your head; add the sound of taxi cabs passing by. Imagine the smell of violets as a street vendor passes while you are seated under a striped umbrella at an outdoor cafe. Feel the warmth of the sun against your back, the roughness of the red and white checkered tablecloth under your elbow. See the white apron of the waiter as he carries a tray of steaming espresso past you to the couple seated at the next table.

Now, look up. There he or she is, standing beside your table, smiling warmly down at you with a hand extended in greeting.

What happens next is up to you. You can invite this person to join you. You can walk away arm and arm; you can jump into a cab for an exciting destination. It is your visualization. Take this opportunity to visualize your hopes and dreams. It is your dream, so you can construct it any way you wish. However, you must create your vision in positive terms, with a happy ending.

Once you've seen it, try drawing it, or find a picture, or create a symbol that represents it.

Once you have clarified your vision, one of the most affecting things you can do to help you realize your dream is a mental rehearsal because this will help you focus on your vision and create positive expectations about the future. The more positive you feel about the future you envision, the more likely it will become a reality.

Write your own affirmation, similar to the one at the end of each chapter—only write one of your very own, one that helps your unique visualization become a positive assertion because this method makes real the future you have imagined. The affirmation, sometimes called positive self-talk, can be achieved by writing out your vision, can be thought silently in your head, or can be spoken aloud. Whatever method you choose, make it in the present tense, as if the man or woman of your dreams already exists in your life. Make it short so that it easy to remember and to repeat over and over. Then do just that, keep repeating it to yourself.

Be patient and watch what happens as you alter your conscious thought and your auric energy.

Carla

Carla works as a proofreader for a small publishing firm. "Even with spell checkers on computers, there are still plenty of errors for a pair of eyes to find," she said. "This is the only job I've ever had. I came here right out of high school and I've been there for nineteen years, with only one more year to go until retirement. I'm looking forward to retiring because I'm not forty yet and I know I can have a whole other career if I want. I just haven't decided what.

"My entire life has been spent alone with women, including my two sisters and my widowed mother, who have been about the extent of my social life," she said. "I even have a female dog and a female cat. I have a parrot I called Michael until he laid an egg, so now I call her Michelle.

"One of the articles I had to proof was about visualization. The man in the article wanted a red Porsche, so he cut a picture out of a magazine, glued it into a notebook, and every day he wrote his affirmation about it on the page beside the picture. He also put a similar picture up at his back door so that every time he went out to get into his car, he saw that red car he wanted instead of the black Nissan parked in his driveway. He said that within six months a car just like it was his! Once he saw that such goal-visualizing worked, he began to do the same for a lot of other things he wanted and they all eventually came to him. The photos that accompanied the article showed him beside a big boat and a fancy house, wearing Gucci shoes. I was intrigued. In my job I read lots of articles about a lot of things, some of them about things I have very little interest in. I forget them in the next five minutes, but this one stayed with me. I thought about what I had read when I got into bed that night and I decided, 'what the heck,' it can't hurt, maybe I'll give it a try.

"It's easy to want material things. If you want them badly enough, you just have to figure out where you can cut back on your other spending, save the money, and some time in the future, whatever it is will be yours. But a husband! That's quite a different goal to visualize. I had a difficult time thinking just how I would go about visualizing a man for myself and then expect him to materialize, like some kind of ghost, before my eyes.

"I'd like to be married, have someone who wants to be with me, who cares about me, someone I could cook for, keep house for, all the usual marriage stuff, but it didn't seem very likely that I'll meet anyone, considering what my dull, routine life has been like.

"I didn't say anything to anyone about this. My family, particularly my mother, they all would have thought I'd gone nuts. I thought about it for quite a while before I began my visualization because I wanted to be sure that I was planning to create someone positive, someone who would be good for me. I decided to make him Latin-looking. You know, dark good looks with pale skin, but other than that I left his physical appearance a little vague. I want someone I can trust, a man who will come home every night after work, someone steady and very reliable, someone intelligent, interested in words. I thought maybe he ought to be a poet or a playwright, that would be someone I would find interesting. I never gave income a thought, that is not very important. The important thing was finding a man who is a decent human being. I got a little notebook and drew a little sketch of my dream man and then I wrote my affirmation and repeated it about him every day as a positive reinforcement.

"After a few months when nothing happened, I have to admit I got a little tired of it all. But by then I had said my affirmation over and over so many times that it had become almost automatic. I would repeat it on the way to work and on the way home, almost like a little tune I was humming in my head.

"When vacation time came around, I didn't have any definite plans and then suddenly a friend from Accounting, Irene Bocelli, asked me if I'd like to go with her to Italy. She had planned to go with a relative, but because of some family problem the other person couldn't go and she was looking for someone to share expenses. I usually don't do things on the spur of the moment, but it was such a bargain that I decided to go with her.

"We had an absolutely fantastic time. It is wonderful to go to a foreign country with someone who speaks the language, knows their way around, and has dozens of relatives in every town. I saw the Vatican in Rome, all the art museums in Florence, the leaning tower of Pisa, and all the usual tourist things, but the best part was staying with Irene's relatives. They were so warm and welcoming. They prepared so much food for us and absolutely wouldn't take 'no' for an answer when they put huge platters of pasta on the table.

"When we got to Genoa, Irene's cousin, Andre, a professor of Byzantine studies at the University, escorted us all over town. You probably can guess that he was dark with pale skin. Andre is a charming gentleman with Old World manners. It wasn't a surprise to me to discover that he wasn't married, because I knew as soon as I saw him that I had been visualizing this very person for months now. I could hardly bring myself to leave when it was time to come home and I know he felt the same way. Is it a fantasy? Am I just hoping for a love-at-first-sight kind of romance novel experience? I hope not. I'm taking it very slowly. I don't want to make a big mistake at forty. We have been corresponding by e-mail daily since I got back and he will be coming to stay with Irene later in the year.

"Everyone tells me how different I am since I came back from my trip. My sisters and my mother all say I'm positively glowing and my outlook on life is so much better. My life has changed. I'm a little hesitant yet to say that I'm in love, but the future looks promising. Will I go to Italy to live? Well, maybe. I'll decide when I see Andre again if that is a goal for me and if it is, you can be sure that I am going to make a little sketch of it, write an affirmation about it in my notebook, and repeat it to myself every day. Why wouldn't I? Just look at what visualization has brought me already!"

Visualizing Your New Friend

Think about the kind of person you wish to come into your life right now: a true friend, a caring lover, perhaps a trustworthy business partner. Write down your choice.

Using whatever name you use when you think of yourself—first name, nickname, not what they call you at work—write an affirmation:

I, _____ deserve to meet a _____ who is _____.

Create a mental picture of this first meeting taking place. Will someone introduce you?

Who? _____ If not, how will you meet? _____

Where _____ Day and date _____

At what time? _____   Weather _____

After the initial greeting, what will you say? _____

Now that you have a clear mental picture of this event occurring, with your *non-dominant hand,* rewrite your affirmation.

As you struggle to write with your other hand, you will possibly find that you are also thinking about reasons why this won't or couldn't possibly happen. For example, I don't *deserve* to meet such a person.

No one will introduce me to a (descriptor from your affirmation) *because* I am _____.

Make a list of possible reasons.

_____
_____
_____
_____

These self-descriptive words, which come from your own subconscious, will be accurate.

Now, with your *non-dominant hand,* rewrite your affirmation using an opposite word. For example, if you wrote: because I am "belligerent," when you rewrite the affirmation, use the word *amiable.* If you wrote: because I am "dull," rewrite the affirmation, stating what you are going *to do* to change that.

I, _____ will meet a _____ who is _____ because I am _____.

This self-description should reveal to you some of the reasons why you have not met the kind of people you desire to be in your life. These words from your own subconscious may be difficult to accept at first, but you can use the opposite and positive word to create a very powerful and life-altering affirmation and you can use it to heal your heart energy and affirm yourself in a positive way daily.

As you reconsider and rewrite your affirmation, you will cleanse and clear your heart chakra of blockage and tension. Visualize a gray cloud surrounding the negative word you used to describe yourself, encompass that image, and move it out from your heart chakra into the atmosphere, making it disappear right into thin air.

Now bring the positive energy from above you in the universe into your heart chakra and let the new positive word flow in with it. Feel warmth in your heart as it enters and brightens up your aura, while you acknowledge and appreciate it.

You have just created a very personal mantra for yourself, a verbal formula that will create a sense of harmony within your heart and that you can repeat often in your meditation.

Tony

Tony, dynamic and handsome, earns his living as a stockbroker, a high-pressure occupation where he handles the accounts of some very wealthy people. He was so disappointed in his love life that he decided that the best thing for him to do was focus all his energy and attention on his career and forget about finding someone to share his life.

"They all just want you to spend money on them, take them places, and buy them gifts. My last girlfriend, Monica, expected flowers every time I saw her!" As he recalled that fact about this last relationship, Tony felt so indignant he had to get up and walk around the room before he could go on. "I don't really need a girl in my life, I'm just fine alone," he exclaimed, but as he said that he began to laugh at himself because, he reluctantly admitted in the next breath, "No, that just isn't true, it's just my anger speaking."

Tony agreed to do the fantasy lover exercise and was a little embarrassed to discover that he found physical appearance to be so important that he often didn't bother with a girl unless she was beautiful and model thin with long straight hair, and she definitely had to be shorter than he was. "Also, I thought my friends would laugh at me if I showed up with someone who didn't fit the image of what people in my business would call 'a high-maintenance woman.' You know," he said sheepishly, "high fashion clothes and well-groomed, someone who would be a reflection of my good taste. I didn't really care about their education just as long as they made me look good. I guess I have to admit that although I'm bright, I'm pretty shallow."

"Looking back at some of my past girlfriends, I can tell you that I've had several relationships that lasted just a few months and in all that time I never knew what their religion was or if they had any at all. While I think those differences can be worked out, I know several mixed-faith couples who didn't seem to have any difficulties in their relationship that I could see until they decided to have children, and then they began to argue about religion. I know I want to avoid that."

He was reluctant to do the wholeness quiz because, as he said after he read it, "That's all arty stuff. I wouldn't light a candle or write poetry." However, he agreed that his decision to focus his attention on his career was exactly the sensitivity-limiting behavior that probably would prevent both his personal growth and his ability to find someone to share his life. After looking over the list of tasks he finally agreed to find a charity in which he could participate, and he would focus on his heart chakra at least once a day with a brief meditation.

Several months later a happy Tony reported, "At first I felt very foolish thinking about my heart and doing the meditation, but I felt that I had agreed, I had made a contract to do it. After a while, I actually began to enjoy it. It was the first time in a long time that I had just sat quietly without doing something, like playing some sport, running a couple of miles to get rid of all my stress, or working out. One evening as I was meditating, an image suddenly came to me in the middle of it. I saw the beach, a particular part of it where I sometimes go with some guys to play volleyball on the weekends. I could see it just the way it looked last Saturday, littered with junk, beer bottles, and fast food wrappers. I usually get furious when I see all the trash left there by tourists, but I have to admit that, although I've resented the way it looks, I never picked up other people's garbage. I got up from my meditation, knowing that I needed to make some changes. I had to do something about how angry that trash all over the sand makes me feel, and I suddenly thought that maybe focusing on my heart chakra wasn't such a silly thing to do after all. I sat right down at my computer, got on the Internet, and found an organization, the Center for Marine Conservation, which conducts an annual International Coastal Cleanup which involves over 35 states, 50 foreign countries, and more than 200,000 volunteers. I couldn't believe that I was volunteering to spend the day picking up stuff along the beach, but I did."

As Tony spoke, his eyes brightened and his shoulders lifted, "They also have a larger mission and I'm a part of that now. It includes working to protect the habitats of whales, dolphins, and sea turtles. On my very first late night trip to the beach to pick up beer cans with this group I saw a loggerhead turtle. I'd never seen one before. They're as big as a car! I got excited about something other than earning money for the first time in years."

Tony hesitated, "I met my new girlfriend that night, too. Her name is Boyza Jane. She's a marine biologist and she's terrific! She doesn't want bouquets of flowers. She wants us to work together to help save the world. She's a Catholic who attends Mass and uses a breviary and a rosary. I was so impressed, I didn't think there were any Catholics that dedicated anymore unless they were from my grandparent's generation. I'm a fallen-away Catholic and she is helping me back to the faith of my childhood and it feels wonderful. I realize now that I was going in the wrong direction with my life, thinking about how to make more and more money, contact richer clients so I could buy more stuff for materialistic girls who want more than I can ever give them. Now Boyza Jane and I belong to the American Hiking Society and we recently went together on a wilderness trip with their Volunteer Vacation program along the Appalachian Trail. Next month we're going with Earthwatch for a two-week study trip to ancient Pompeii."

Tony laughed, "My heart chakra is opening and getting all charged up. I'm going in the right direction now and Boyza Jane tells me my aura looks great!"

M.K.

M.K. is a short, slender girl with her hair curling gently around her face. "My initials don't stand for anything," she said. "It is fairly common in the South to give people initials for their name. I used to have a lot of fun with it because most people assume they are going to meet a man when they read my name, and I have enjoyed their surprise when I show up.

"I got a job in an insurance office right out of high school and I started going to the local community college at night. I was dating my high school sweetheart, Phil, and it looked to me like my life was all set. I planned to get a degree in something like accounting, marry Phil, have a couple of kids, and live happily ever after.

"Somehow the college got my classes mixed up with someone who had my same last name and initials, and I ended up finding out that I was enrolled in some engineering classes. I thought it would take a couple of days before it got straightened out so I went to the first classes. I was amazed to find that I absolutely loved it. Engineering was not something I had ever thought about before. The courses were filled with men and a lot of them had plans to get jobs working for NASA on the space program after they got their degrees. In one of these first classes I met Robert and my 'happily ever after' plan for my life went right out the window.

"I didn't really believe in love at first sight, but wow! Robert was everything any woman could ever imagine. He was soap-opera handsome, tall and athletic, with the most beautiful blue eyes I have ever seen, a great laugh, and the most good-looking smile. The great part of it was that he didn't seem to have any idea how gorgeous he was. I got goose bumps all over whenever he walked into the room.

"Well, to make a long story short, I broke up with Phil, went to live with Robert, and learned the hard way that I had fallen in love with a facade, not a real person. Robert was so alluring, so persuasive, his personality was so magnetic that I couldn't think, even in my wildest dreams, that he was absolutely emotionless and ruthless. He is so manipulative and scheming that even to this day, it is difficult for me to realize how truly deceptive and fake both his personality and his behavior were. I found out later that even before I moved in with him, while we were dating, he was seeing two other girls. He had been married twice and had a child from his first marriage whom he never saw, didn't support, and just 'forgot' to mention! I realize now that Robert is a con artist, someone I always saw stories about on TV. I never thought I could be taken by someone like him. I know now that I 'fell in love with love' and it has taken a lot of hard work on my part to realize that Robert was just a symptom of how dull the life I had planned for myself really was.

"My engineering degree has made it possible for me to work in robotics now, and I'm very thankful for that. It is a career with a future in a lot of industries, including the movies. I'm not sure where Robert is today, but the last I knew he was installing fancy car radios in expensive cars and using his work to meet women who have credit cards he can run up.

"For quite a while I was desolate. I thought I had ruined my life, but I've been trying to do some of the Wholeness Tasks and while some of them seem very simple, they have opened my eyes to the fact that I was really limiting myself. I started listening to Mozart and that interested me so much that I began taking piano lessons. The engineer part of me understands and enjoys the complexity of the mathematical structure of music. I have begun to think that my healing heart can perhaps write music sometime soon. Just last year my grandmother was sick and now she lives in a nursing home. I have been going there on the weekends to visit her, playing the piano for her and the other residents and I've found that to be very therapeutic, not just for them but for me, too. It is very rewarding to see how much they enjoy live music. I've had to learn a lot of old tunes, Glen Miller and Tommy Dorsey things, all the music that they love from the Big Band era. After I perform for them, they come up and hug me and thank me and tell me stories about their youth. I've heard lots of tales about their romances and marriages and it seems to help them to tell me these things.

"I loved Robert for all the wrong reasons. My relationship with him was unhealthy and unfulfilling, and I am working now, creating a strong and vibrant aura so that someone who is honest and real will be guided to me."

Heart Chakra Tasks

Burn some jasmine incense.

Eat a piece of fruit. Imagine the person who picked it and sent it on its way for you.

Recall a favorite pet from your childhood, say its name, and picture it in your mind.

Do a small kindness for a stranger or a friend.

Recall the first time you sent or received flowers. To or from whom?

Visit an aquarium.

Observe and learn from the trees in the forest. They know how to patiently wait.

Visualization

As you think about the limitations you may have put on your heart and the love you are willing to give to others, visualize your heart chakra extending outward in a broad field of green, the color of compassion. See this energy expanding to encompass not only yourself but others in the world who may be less fortunate than you and who would be grateful to have even the smallest amount of your graciousness and empathy. See your heart chakra expanding and bringing into your own life whose hearts are brimming with generosity and humanitarianism, while you leave behind fear and disappointment.

Close your eyes and bathe in a soft green healing light those who have angered you by mean, selfish, or cruel behavior. Deep in a forest see a celestial wishing tree in front of you; from its branches dangle the deepest wishes of your heart. The warm air of a summer evening gently rocks the branches and releases those heartfelt wishes to the clouds, up to the power of the universe that will return them to you. Wait patiently and you will see.

Heart Chakra Meditation

> "As I breathe in, my heart expands to include those who need love,
> As I exhale, I leave behind all those who cannot care,
> My heart beats in rhythm with my heart's desire.
> I am connected to the bountiful hearts of those in my future."

Heart Chakra Affirmation

> "I choose to let the energy from the universe make my heart chakra unfold like a blossom as I open myself to accept inner peace."
> "I choose to meet a lover who has a generous and loving heart."
> "I choose to let my positive affirmation become a self-fulfilling prophecy."

Heart Chakra Future

As you become more generous and kind, friends and lovers who are generous and compassionate will begin to enter your life. Wait. Open your heart and such friends will arrive from places unknown to you now and they will appear most unexpectedly. Look around, you may be surprised.

9 Heal How and What You Communicate

The tongue is the only tool that
gets sharper with use.

—Washington Irving

Fifty years ago you could travel along any street or country road at the end of the day and see couples sitting together on their front porches, often rocking back and forth in unison as they rested in big comfortable chairs. Or, you might see them sitting side by side in a porch swing that hung from the rafters, their arms touching, speaking softly to each other, sometimes singing familiar songs. Often you might see young couples with children at their feet and older couples with their hands folded across ample bellies, with perhaps a dog or two resting lazily on the stairs. People gazed at the setting sun and talked to each other, reflecting on the accomplishments or the difficulties of the day.

Psychobiologist Ernest Lawrence Rossi feels that, more than just resting together at the end of the day, these couples were synchronizing their circadian and ultradian rhythms. Often they needed no more than five minutes at the end of the day to get in synch with each other. Researchers believe that intimate relations are tied to a kaleidoscope of biological forces. A shared quiet time helped lower stress levels and reduce the odds that tensions or frustrations would be allowed to grow. In addition to synchronizing their biological rhythms, these couples were connecting through the invisible energy of their auras, allowing their heart strings to be continuously intertwined in a love knot of mutual caring, sharing, and understanding.

Only the romantics among us believe that a loving relationship is suddenly discovered, not built over time. Experts now say that lasting love and the deep, often exhilarating shared experiences of intimacy and romance are actually born and sustained by innumerable small and varied events that are experienced and shared between two people.

Worlds Apart

As the world has grown smaller and smaller, people now have the ability to move quickly and easily around the globe. Young and old can live far away from the traditions and people they have known all their lives. Today we can find ourselves meeting people from many new and different cultures and while telecommunications, television, and commercial jet travel appear to be making global interactions easier, they have increased the complexity of what we have to know to appreciate and understand each other.

All over the world there was a time when family units were much more closely connected and structured. In the past children would not even consider disobeying the rules of their families. It was expected that families would select wives and husbands for their children. It was traditionally thought that parents understood what was needed to match the individual personalities and traits of their children There were family and tribal connections to be made through these marriages, which extended far beyond the needs of the children involved, and everyone understood and accepted their assigned roles in these links. The concept of arranged marriages was often part of a common tradition established for so long that it had achieved the force or validity of law. These cultural and tribal laws were understood and accepted by everyone. Commonly held beliefs made most of these families far more cohesive than the modern family is today. It was understood and accepted that parents and community elders knew the needs of their children and the community far better than any of the future brides and grooms—who were often no more than relative strangers.

Couples in India today who have been married by these ancient customs often state that, although they might not have chosen the partner for themselves that their families selected for them, they respect this wisdom enough to accept that it is their job to work through the early stages of such a planned marriage. In interviews many of these couples say they now believe they are in love with their husband or wife and are settled and secure in a relationship that will be viable for life. When people come from similar cultures, it is much easier for these couples to possess shared activity patterns, appetites, needs for diversion, and sexual rhythms.

Would such a system work in the United States today? Probably not, for a variety of reasons, including the diverse ethnic backgrounds of the population. Yet surely more wisdom could be used in selecting a life partner than the emotional joining of many modern couples, resulting in relationships that often end in divorce and bitterness rather than happiness and joy.

Today, young people often live in cities far from their families. They meet each other in bars or at the office, are introduced to each other by friends rather than parents, then spend some brief time together, and decide that they find each other sexy instead of interesting. These relationships are often based on physical attraction and not much else. Love affairs with relative strangers frequently go sour because, when the time comes to talk about what they really want and how to handle their problems, these two people find they neither understand nor are able to communicate with each other. Modern lifestyles seem to require that both partners in the relationship work. Once these young people move in together, their lives soon become a merry-go-round. They find they are rushing home, hurrying to prepare dinner, flipping through the newspaper, eating quickly, and then either collapsing for the evening in front of the television or plunging into another round of scheduled activities such as nightly errands, exercise sessions, parental duties, paperwork, preparing reports, or paying bills. Such a harried life allows people no time to unplug from the commotion of the day and sit together quietly, without television and without further tasks and chores. These couples are unable to enter into each other's energy rhythms and recover together from the day's grinding pace. It is no surprise that of the relationships that last until marriage, more than 50 percent of those end in divorce.

Communication

The fifth or throat chakra, which is located at the thyroid gland, is considered the communication chakra. It is the one where your ability to create language, to express yourself, and to understand the words of others is housed.

The four chakras, from the root to the heart, have been given a connection by ancient cultures to the elements of the earth—earth, water, fire, and air. Later experts have suggested "sound" as the "element" for the fifth chakra because it is through the throat that we produce the vibrations that allow us to communicate and express ourselves. It is the source of more than communication, however. That is where we take in nourishment in a variety of forms—food, nurturing, caring—as well as give nourishment to others.

A weak fifth chakra will attract those who are glib and deceitful, who can easily manipulate others, and often results in someone who uses food or drugs to cover emotional anguish and avoid the pain involved in working through some of the difficulties of life. A strong fifth chakra brings the ability to express your feelings and let others know what you really want, as well as strengthening individual self-reliance.

Talking to a Stranger

Pretend that by chance you have met a very attractive someone in a bookstore, in a restaurant, or at a sporting event. No one introduced you; you know no one in common. After chatting briefly, you decide to go for coffee or a drink and get better acquainted.

You've been without a significant other for a quite a while and you are tired of dating. Anxious to avoid spoiling what appears to be a promising potential relationship, you are determined to see if this could turn out to be a fortunate new beginning.

1. You notice a white line on his or her ring finger. Do you:
   Ignore it _____ Joke about it _____ Ask directly _____

2. This stranger asks about your job, but you aren't working at the moment. Do you:
   Change the subject _____ Joke about it _____ Answer honestly _____

3. You observe that your new acquaintance has dirty fingernails and fairly unkempt hair. Do you:
   Ignore it _____ Joke about it _____ Look for other self-esteem clues _____

4. After you chat for a while, this potential partner begins to complain about his or her last relationship. Do you:
   Ask questions _____ Feel sympathetic _____ Complain about yours _____

5. He or she talks about alcohol, drugs, and exploits with "party" friends. Do you:
   Ask questions _____ Agree to party _____ Change the subject _____

6. As you talk, his or her eyes rove to every attractive passerby. Do you:
   Ignore it _____ Joke about it _____ Do the same _____

7. As you walk together to your cars, you notice a not-so-funny bumper sticker and you are told it was on the car when it was purchased. Do you:
   Ignore it _____ Joke about it _____ Ask directly _____

8. After spending half an hour with this new acquaintance and noticing a number of clues that tell you this is not the person for you. Do you:
Exchange phone numbers anyway _____   Promise to get together again _____   Say a pleasant but firm goodbye _____

Take a look at your answers and see if you are willing to ignore obvious clues that this relationship would not be good for you because you think (a) they are only minor problems that can be "worked out" later or (b) because you don't wish to hurt this new person's feelings.

There are three ways to respond to these questions, with varying levels of intensity: passively, aggressively, and assertively. Only the latter is good for healing your chakra and setting you on the path of a trustful and honest relationship.

If you avoided or ignored something that was obviously a problem, you are being too passive in the very beginning of such a relationship. You are keeping this chakra closed down and limiting your ability to communicate.

If you joked about it, you are being passive-aggressive, another not-so-good way to communicate your real opinions. Jokes can point out the problem and possibly soften the impact of the difficulty the remark can create, but they can also backfire. While you can always say, "I was just joking," you got your point across in a passive-aggressive manner while still giving yourself the option of appearing to accept the answer. You are blocking this chakra and making any communication convoluted, with the potential for misunderstanding.

If your question provoked an angry or annoyed reply and then you responded in kind, that is aggressive behavior. This is the worst of all for creating a working and beautiful chakra.

If you asked a direct question and found that you got an evasive answer or one that you didn't like, now is the time to be assertive and truthful.

Do you have the courage to say something like, "I've enjoyed our short time together but I don't think this relationship will be beneficial for either of us"? If you have dealt directly with potential problems because you didn't like the answers to the questions, you could possibly be on the road to an honest relationship. You might be quite surprised, the kind of answers an assertive and direct question could bring. An honest and trustful relationship could be the result. What a lot of heartache and disappointment this would save for both parties. In addition, such honesty will unblock the throat chakra and make it spin and whirl beautifully, just as it is supposed to do.

Communication is more than words. A great deal of suffering could be avoided by paying attention to all the clues that are there at the beginning of any relationship. If you see an obvious clue but are afraid to question it, or are hesitant that you might anger your new acquaintance, or are so needy that you are willing to ignore something that means trouble, perhaps you need to work more on your ability to communicate directly and openly before you think about starting any new relationship. As you become more honest and direct in your communication skills, your throat chakra will also become more open and healed, making it possible for you to avoid the problems that come from dishonest communications.

Talking to a Friend

"Have another beer."

"Come on, it's a party."

"You aren't going to wear that, are you?"

"Just meet this guy, I promise you, he's different."

"You don't want to take that class, it will be boring."

"Oh, just one bite won't hurt you."

"Don't be a wet blanket."

We've all heard variations on these statements from our friends. While most of us would like to think that we make our own decisions about what we are going to do or not do, we all succumb at one time or another to peer pressure. It doesn't matter how old you are or how experienced, your friends can often encourage you to do things you know you shouldn't do, really don't want to do. They can help you to either feel better about behavioral decisions you have made or cause you to experience emotional damage and possible later regrets.

List five friends with whom you spend time or do things on a regular basis:

_____   _____   _____   _____   _____

Answer the following:

1. Do any of them encourage you to drink, party, or drive too fast when you really don't want to, just so they will have company? Yes___ No___

2. Do any of them encourage you to eat the wrong foods, forgo exercising, or stay out late on a work night? Yes___ No___

3. Do any of them want you to go to clubs to meet guys or girls just because they are lonely? Yes___ No___

4. Do you secretly think maybe some of these friends have a drinking or a drug habit? Yes___ No___

5. Do any of them encourage you to go shopping and buy expensive things you can't really afford? Yes___ No___

6. Do any of them repeat harmful gossip they heard about you to you? Yes___ No___

7. Do any of them discourage you from making career changes because it might reflect badly on their inability to move on? Yes___ No___

8. Do any of them make plans to meet you at certain time and place and then never show up? Yes___ No___

9. Do any of them expect special treatment so they will know they are your "best" friend? Yes___ No___

10. Do any of them lie regularly, and you know it? Yes___ No___

11. Do any of them borrow, money, clothes, tools, and never re-
    turn them?   Yes___ No___

12. Do any of them lose things, create an uproar about it, and
    then blame you?   Yes___ No___

13. Do you sometimes think they are hardly worth the trouble?
    Yes___ No___

14. Do they make statements like "everyone's doing it" to get you
    to go along?   Yes___ No___

Some of our friends are often our friends for the very worst of
reasons. Frequently, they are charismatic, creative, with powerful
ideas, strongly convincing—and lots and lots of fun.

If you have more than five "Yes" answers, you may need to
examine whether these people are really the kind of friends you
need. These individuals have their own auras projecting their
energy into the universe and, since we cannot avoid coming into contact with their energy, their aura, it is important to examine just how truly beneficial these people are for you. You may
come to the realization that not only is their negative and destructive energy impinging on your aura, they may be actually
drawing energy from you for their own use. It is important to
surround yourself with people who have positive and beneficial
energy.

Talking to a Real Friend

Another kind of peer pressure comes from people who share your
values, help you feel good about achievements, encourage you to
do new things, and challenge you to try harder when you want
to quit. Sometimes your peers can be the most important social
forces in your life, particularly if they help you overcome fear of
failure and loneliness, and reinforce you when you want to explore
new friendships and new ideas.

Value and cherish those people in your life who treat you with kindness and nurture your heart, who hold you dear, who help and support you.

If you come to the realization that you need to drop negative and destructive people from your circle, know that the universe has brought to you to this awareness and it has something or someone better in store for you.

Tiffany

Tiffany, slim, with an athletic grace, works in a small kiosk selling designer sunglasses in the center of the mall. "Everyone thinks it's a great place to meet men because they tend to buy lots of expensive sunglasses, but it isn't really. You only see them for about fifteen minutes and then they are gone. My friend Crystal works in the mall, too, in one of the big department stores, and we do lots of things together. One of the problems is that we have different hours, conflicting schedules, because the mall stores are open seven days a week and late at night. So sometimes one of us comes in late in the afternoon while the other one came to work in the morning. When she works late and I work early, I'll come back and pick her up and we'll go out after 11 at night.

"We often go to a country-western bar and they really get pretty exciting after midnight. One of the dances they do makes it possible for you to dance with different people for a few minutes at a time. Some places call it a barn dance; others call it a wild, wild west. The way it works is you begin dancing with one partner and then the caller calls out for the men to shift. The women stay in place and the men move to the next partner. Even on a busy night you can meet almost every man in the place. Crystal really loves it. She is so anxious to meet somebody, to get married, to find romance. I keep telling her that she isn't going to find the man of her dreams in a country-western bar, but she likes those guys in snakeskin boots with big silver buckles on their belts."

Tiffany shook her long hair as she thought about it. "Sometimes I tell her I'm not going to go with her anymore. Sometimes she leaves me alone in the place. I don't even know she is gone until I start looking for her so we can leave. She will go home with some guy she just met there that night and when I try to tell her that is too dangerous, she just changes the subject. You know what happens next? She'll call me to come pick her up from wherever she spent the night so she can get to work. If I tell her I can't do it, she starts crying and makes me feel so guilty that I give in to her. I know I should probably stop seeing Crystal, but I don't seem to be able to. I always think about how much fun she can be when it's just the two of us. We laugh and laugh and she is so lively and so full of mischief, that I can't wait to see what she is going to do next. I tell myself over and over that I'm not going to go with her anymore, but I always do. She can seduce me right into the same trap of thinking we are going to have a lot of fun, we are going to meet interesting men, that our lives are going to change, over and over again. And you know what? Nothing changes.

"I know I have to become stronger in letting Crystal know how I feel and that I want to do something different. I'm just not communicating with her when it comes to speaking up and saying I don't want to go to those dumpy places any more. I've got to be stronger, firmer, saying that the two of us have to change our ways if we are really ever going to meet a reliable man, somebody worth doing more with than sashaying around a sawdust-covered floor."

Although Tiffany doesn't know it yet, her fifth chakra is very weak, making her a pushover for her glib and controlling friend. However, just talking about how she is feeling, realizing that she needs to get different friends, friends who will recognize that she is a valuable individual, reliable, trustworthy, and bright, friends who will not pressure her or make her feel guilty if she doesn't do things their way, may be the beginning of her realizing the need for change.

Syncronicity may provide her with a serendipitous coincidence, too, because the energy of the universe has seen to it that she is going to get something she needs. For Christmas her grandmother's gift to her will be a book about auras, along with a turquoise ring and a stick of frankincense.

Talking to Yourself

The throat chakra is about more than communication; it is also about nurturing your relationships as well as yourself. Often we take better care of others than we do of ourselves.

Answer the following:

1. How do you feel today? If you are working hard, reward yourself with some small pleasure. If you are tired, take a short break.

2. Are you eating well?   Yes___   No___
   If you are not feeding your body as well as your soul, you cannot progress. Take the time to have a good meal, a nourishing snack, and some food for thought.

3. Do you have something new to wear?   Yes___   No___
   If you haven't bought yourself something new for a while, make a small purchase such as stockings, a tie, or a scarf.

4. Have you taken the time for some solitude?   Yes___   No___
   Solitude is different than being alone. Sit with some soft music and your thoughts, take a few deep breaths, and relax with your eyes closed and your shoes off.

5. Is there something you wish you owned but don't?
   Yes___   No___
   Name it. Say it out loud. Once it is named, find a photograph of whatever it is and put it up on your bathroom mirror. Allow your energy to flow toward receiving it when you look at yourself in the mirror in the morning. You will be amazed, because if it is right for you, the energy that you are projecting will come back from the universe and the universe will bring it to you.

Finding the Marrying Kind

Perhaps you think you may have found someone with potential for a permanent relationship, because you feel comfortable with this person. Or you have decided you will be smarter and more observant about the vibrations you get from any new relationship. Answer the following:

1. Have you known him or her for *at least* one year?
   Yes___ No___
   If your answer to this questions is "no," it might be wise to wait and give yourself an opportunity to see this individual in action in a greater variety of situations.

2. Is he or she affectionate with his or her mother and father?
   Yes___ No___

3. Is he or she respectful of his or her siblings?   Yes___ No___

4. What is the mood at a family get together?
   Joyful?___ Tense?___

5. Are his or her parents divorced?   Yes___ No___

6. Are there relatives with commitment issues, drug or alcohol issues? Yes___ No___
   If you have never met any of his or her family and don't know the answers to some of these questions, it might be a good idea to arrange to meet them. This is one of the best indicators of the future because we are supposed to learn what relationships are like from our family. If this family is dysfunctional, remember, this is where he or she learned what relationships and marriage are meant to be like.

7. Did he or she have any long-term relationships before meeting you?   Yes___ No___

8. Have you heard his or her explanation of what caused them to part?   Yes___ No___

If it is all the other's fault, you'd better ask a lot of questions now.

9. Are there one-night stands in her or his past?   Yes___   No___
   If you don't know the answers to these questions, perhaps you'd better find out, because your friend may only be saying she or he is ready for a long-term commitment.

10. Can you talk to each other for hours at a time?   Yes___   No___

11. Is your relationship based on exciting sex and when you have to spend other time together, are there awkward silences? Yes___   No___

12. Can your new friend tell you how he or she is feeling? Yes___   No___

13. Do you know how your friend reacts to setbacks, such as a job loss or an illness?   Yes___   No___

14. Are you able to discuss the future? Have you talked about such topics as children, financial security, who will maintain the checkbook, retirement living, or what you would do if you had to take care of an elderly or ill parent?   Yes___   No___

15. Do you think, "My friend would be perfect if only he or she would _____." (Fill in the blank.)
    If you are able to fill in that blank easily, this relationship is headed for trouble. Thinking that love can change anything about someone (other than their wardrobe) is a delusion.

16. Have you seen your friend *really* angry?   Yes___   No___
    If not, this might be a wise thing, although unpleasant, to see. It could be an important clue about what to expect in the future.

If you don't have a committed relationship at the moment, some of these questions may help you to realize that before you become too involved with someone, you need to communicate honestly about intimate and important issues.

A Creative Imaginary Life

Most of us have looked back with regret at the lives we chose—
our marriages, careers, or other destinations. If you do look back,
you can see there was a fork in the road where you made a decision that, at the time, didn't seem to make that much difference in
where you would end up. If you decided you were bored with
school and dropped out before high school graduation, obviously
that has limited your career choices. Did a friend offer you a job
in his business and while it didn't interest you much, it was easy,
so you took it? Did the town you lived in have very little in the
way of businesses that would offer a future, but you took something to stay near your current love interest and then never moved
on? Did your family members expect you to follow in their foot-
steps and you didn't want to disappoint? Did you meet somebody
interesting at school and change your major to be in more classes
with him or her?

Have you often thought that if only you had done something
different, you might have met different people, had a different career,
gone a different route, lived a different life? If you haven't, you are
pretty unusual.

The president of a high-powered placement service says, Many
people are living lives of quiet desperation, saying "I've got to get
out of this situation," but frequently they never do. One-third of employed, college-educated adults surveyed by the Gallup Organization
said they would, if given the chance to start all over again, opt for
a different line of work and 10 percent of Americans actually switch
occupations every year, according to the Bureau of Labor Statistics.

Answer the following:

1. What was your career goal in high school?

   _____

2. Did you take the right steps to follow that choice?
   Yes___ No___

3. If you could have taken a different path, what would you be
   now? List five possible careers paths that you might have

chosen. (Example: police officer, doctor, teacher, scientist, sculptor, classical guitarist, pilot, playwright, telephone repairman.)

———————   ———————   ———————   ———————   ———————

4. Look over your list and select one. Write a brief paragraph about how your life would have been different. (Example: If I had become a college professor, I would be associating with intellectually stimulating people. If I had become a painter, I would be meeting patrons of the arts. If I had become a pilot, I would be finding romance in foreign lands.)

———————————————————————————————————————
———————————————————————————————————————
———————————————————————————————————————

Shifting to a new career rarely turns out to be the burn-your-bridges-behind-you act that you might expect. Frederick Williams, a counselor at a career action center, says, "People often assume that everything is wrong; that they will have to throw everything away, start all over again, go back to school, go into debt, learn a whole set of new skills. But that simply isn't true. Changing careers is not about dramatic change. It's about continuity, about translating your experience and your expertise into transferable, marketable skills."

5. If you think you can improve your life or find more interesting and positive relationships by a career or occupation change, list one skill that you have or can acquire that an individual with the career you named in number 4 has.

———————————————————————————————————————

(Example: guitarist—you can learn to play or practice so that you improve, join a pickup band or a group; police officer—learn to shoot, become an expert marksman, take classes in police science; doctor—acquire a medical vocabulary, study basic anatomy; teacher—read up on one subject until you are an expert, volunteer at a local school as an aide; sculptor—take art classes, work with clay, learn how to fire and glaze ceramics.)

Thinking about the benefits of a career change can be a challenging and courageous idea. If you think your life would be improved by coming closer to making such a change, or merely imagine that acquiring some of the skills such a career entails would make you happier, then do just that and see how it feels. Perhaps you think that your alternative choices are impossible, would take too much time, would be too difficult, or that it's too late, but if you are willing to take a few small steps toward the goal of realizing your dream, you might learn that it is not as implausible as you first thought. Perhaps you might discover that you are now interesting and attractive to a whole new group of people because by making these changes you have automatically altered your aura. Now you have a new skill, new knowledge; you have discovered and exercised some untapped talent that was actually lying dormant, waiting for you to vitalize your aura with the right energy.

Just bringing this information into your consciousness will recharge your chakra and bring you closer to the stability created by a fully activated aura.

Stanley

Stanley was quite successful; he had a good job as a vice president of a substantial lumber company in Washington state, but he wasn't happy. "I was so busy, going to meetings, taking work home in the evening, flying around the country to meet with builders, that I had no time for a social life at all. Everyone assumed that my life was exciting, dramatic, and filled with adventure. People who knew me would ask if I had met any beautiful flight attendants lately, or if I was dating any New York show girls. Nobody seemed to think I might be lonely. I never had time to go to any New York shows, never mind meet anyone performing in them. Brief meetings of attractive women, such as on a plane or at the reception desk at corporate offices, had almost zero potential for connecting with someone and developing that brief contact into any kind of a relationship.

"I don't make big bucks anymore. I don't travel a lot, and I don't negotiate complicated deals or live in a wonderful dream house."

Two years ago Stanley gave it all up to teach eighth grade history in a suburb of Seattle. He had to cut way back on how he lives, and he still has to work for a paycheck.

"I get a real kick out of teaching. I went on a bus with my kids to the state capitol for a conference on government and had a wonderful time. I now spend some of my free time singing in a church choir, something I never had time for before. I've got a woodworking set up in my garage and I'm building furniture for my TV room. A committee at my church asked if I'd build some furniture for a shelter they are funding, and I'll probably do that. I know I'm happier and more relaxed now than I've been in years.

"I guess perhaps my change in attitude from that hard-driving SOB I used to be has paid off in other ways, too. Recently a corporate friend invited me over to his house for dinner and they had another guest there, a librarian named Martha. They had invited her specifically so that the two of us could meet. My friend said, 'We could never have introduced you to Martha when you were still working at the company. She wouldn't have liked the person you were then and you probably wouldn't have taken the time to talk to her more than once.' I know now that I had lost any enthusiasm I might have had for the lumber business a long time ago. In hindsight, I realize that I had been on a treadmill for a very long time. I never had time for a vacation; my free time was always interrupted because of corporate crises, and I was never home to enjoy all that my hard work had brought me.

"Martha is a wonderful woman and we spent a lot of time together, getting to know each other, learning about each other's lives. We can sit by the fireplace at Martha's cottage and I listen to music while she knits for hours at a time. Martha has several cats, animals I never could tolerate before, but I'm learning to understand them because I realize you have to sit quietly and wait for them to finish checking you out before they accept you. Martha says animals read auras and I believe her. Sitting quietly is something I guess I'm finally learning to do."

Sabotaging Self-Talk

We always talk to ourselves in our heads. As you drive your car, perform chores around the house, sit at your desk or on the job, any time you appear to be silent, it is only an appearance, because you are silently talking in your mind, to your self, about yourself.

Circle the things you have told yourself recently:

1. I'm just a failure.
2. Men/women get bored with me pretty easily.
3. I'm not pretty/handsome enough. Or I'm too _____ (fat, thin, tall, short).
4. It's too late for me.
5. I always say the wrong thing.
6. I'm too needy and it shows.
7. I've done a lot of things I'm ashamed of.
8. How could I have been so stupid (dumb, silly, crazy)?
9. Sometimes I wonder if I'm going crazy.
10. I just don't know how to: (dress, dance, sail, ski, talk, write).
11. I'm over/under sexed.
12. I'm too irresponsible.
13. I can never stay faithful for long.
14. I just know I'll end up all alone.
15. My parents think no one is good enough for me.
16. If only I had _____ (kept quiet, spoken up, laughed, walked away).
17. Why can't I _____ (tell the truth, avoid answering, go out, stay home).
18. I guess he or she will never (call, smile at me, talk to me).
19. (add your own)
20. (add your own)

You can probably add a few to the list. However, you can be sure that these negative thoughts have probably occurred to almost everyone on the planet, including movie stars, sports heroes, and lots of other people you think have incredibly successful lives.

Look at the items you have circled and rewrite each one in a positive mode. (Example: "I am a success at _____." "People find me interesting when I _____." "I have beautiful _____."

Every time you begin to think one of these negative thoughts, you must mentally say to yourself, "Stop!" Then rewrite the thought in a positive mode in your head, and if you are someplace where you can do it, also write it out so that you can see it, feel it, and think it to believe it.

Wendy

With tears in her eyes, Wendy said, "I am one of those women about whom it is often said, 'But she has such a pretty face.' I know people say that about me. At the same time they are shaking their heads in dismay about how overweight I am. Even some of my very good friends have unexpectedly said hurtful things to me while they thought they were being helpful. They've suggested things I could wear that would make me look slimmer or asked if I wanted to sit at a table rather than in a booth, 'It might be a tight squeeze for you.' I know what they mean. What they really want to say is, 'Don't be such a pig. Lose weight. We're embarrassed to be seen with you.'

"My weight has fluctuated over the years. When I'm happy, I'm slim and when I'm unhappy. . . . " Wendy paused. "Well, I'd hate to tell you how heavy I've been, but let me just say there have been times when I have been very, very unhappy.

"I've had several relationships in the past couple of years. There was Ed and then Fred and I always laugh and say I guess I'll just have to find Ted next. But now that I have examined my relationship with both Ed and Fred in an overall perspective—that is, instead of just looking at what was wrong with each one, I've examined them both at the same time so I could get a kind of an overview. I've always known that I am attracted to very low-key men, guys who are very quiet. I've always enjoyed men who want to stay home and work around the house, and then I get angry when I have drag them out and force them to have conversations, even with their own friends. I've made the mistake of wanting to believe that a quiet man was thinking lofty and romantic thoughts, was deeply introspective, and even when it became obvious to me that it wasn't so, I wanted to keep on believing it. I'm very outgoing and talkative. I love having friends over or going out with groups of people. I'm always laughing and singing, expressing myself in painting and drawing. Although there was a different reason for each of these relationships ending, ultimately it always came down to the same thing—a lack of communication. Each one of my relationships have been with the same type of guy, and I guess I thought that sort of balanced me, because I am pretty loud a lot of the time. Now I'm wondering how I got involved with them in the first place.

"Since I began to think about my fifth chakra, I realized that while I am talkative and love to joke around, I am unable to speak about the things that are troubling me in a relationship. When a relationship would be going bad, I simply could not communicate my thoughts or feelings and would begin to eat to soothe myself. I would fall into a vicious cycle of not communicating, feeling unloved and unhappy, and then I would just begin bingeing. That would usually be the end of the relationship because even a guy who likes plump women usually draws the line somewhere.

"Now that I've become much more aware of auras, I know that I usually sensed something I didn't really like about the men that I've been in relationships with, but I pushed it away because I didn't want to know about it or see it. I wanted them to be my romantic, idealized man, not the real person they were. I know I must work on my ability to communicate and I've been making an honest effort to tell people how I feel instead of joking my way around life. I don't plan a career as a fat-girl standup comic. When I really communicate my feelings, then I don't have to get so loud and obnoxious. I don't have to fill the silence with jokes.

"I believe the major thing that has been out of balance in my life is my lack of understanding of how and what I was communicating. I thought I was great at it because I talked so much, but now I realize that I was saying nothing. I totally ignored nonverbal communication, like listening, touch, and body language. And by not communicating with me verbally, my boyfriends were really saying a lot by not listening, avoiding physical contact with me, and turning away or just ignoring me.

"The result of my realization that my throat chakra was really blocked is that I've been attempting to be more honest with everybody, including my coworkers and my friends. I've been attempting to be more honest with everybody about my feelings. When I don't have to choke back my emotions, when I don't repress my tears and stifle my thoughts, I've been able to be far more open and direct, without having to make fun of something to get my point across. Finally, I've been able to get my weight under control for the first time in my life. Isn't that something?!"

Roy

Roy is a talk show host on a local pop music station. "My job is to read commercials and talk, talk, talk, all day long. I am the host of what is known as a drive hour in the late afternoon. It is slanted to people getting off work and heading home in their cars. People can call in and talk for a minute or two about almost anything. Usually, they want to complain about their boss or the traffic or some current event, and it's my job to keep it moving, entertaining, and funny—sometimes funny and entertaining is at the expense of the feelings of the caller. Funny put-downs, corny jokes, and embarrassing questions have been my signature.

"Every celebrity I've ever interviewed has talked about the groupies they have and how they just got tired of all this easy sex that was available to them and how lonely they really are. When you are considered some kind of a celebrity, even if its only a radio personality, you don't have much of a problem finding beautiful girls to go out with you, beautiful girls who want to go to bed with you. I've met lots of flashy, crazy, willing-to-do-almost anything girls, and, just like people a lot more famous than myself, I was getting very tired of that whole scene. These relationships always started out being exciting and powerfully sexy but ended up by my discovering they were just shallow and self-absorbed women who soon grew tired of me, too, when they discovered that life with me wasn't all premieres, concerts, back stage passes, and parties.

"When I met DeeDee, you could say it was love at first sight, at least on my part. I couldn't believe how beautiful and nice she was. She was the organizer at a charity event that I was asked to MC. She had never heard my program and didn't seem to know who I was, but she was polite and friendly without going overboard about meeting someone in the media. I was amazed to find myself fascinated by a real person. This was a girl I was really interested in getting to know better. We'd talk on the phone late at night and, although I was really attracted to her, I began to realize that, because she was a distant voice over the telephone, just like a caller on my radio show, I could easily drift into that radio persona. People who listen to my show love my easygoing, slick way of communicating, and I was absolutely floored when it didn't attract DeeDee at all. We dated for a while. We went dancing and out to dinner and a few clubs, but after no more than a few months DeeDee began to be busy when I called. Although she was courteous, I knew she was trying to let me down easy.

"Although it is a loosely kept secret, I guess most people know that drugs are easy to come by in the entertainment industry. I'd often show up for work stoned and I had come to believe that a few drinks before I went on the air made me a little more free, got my creative juices going. I had problems, though, because my drinking often caused me to have temperamental rages—I'd call them 'creative differences'—with management, because I thought of myself as some kind of an artist, but in reality I was just out of control a lot of the time. I often had a little coke or a drink before taking DeeDee out and that had never been a problem with any of the other women I had dated. In fact, when they knew I could get coke, they were even more interested in me than they had been before, particularly the models, who needed to keep their weight under control.

"When DeeDee told me that I was 'glib, insincere, and a superficial druggie,' I was stunned. I considered myself the silver-tongued darling of talk and I never dreamed that anyone could see any difference in me when I was using. I could hardly believe that she could think such things, never mind say it to me. I was so angry with her that, for once, I couldn't think of anything to say. However, when DeeDee walked away from me, I had to take a good hard look at myself. I made a very good living being glib, insincere, and superficial, but I was almost forced to consider that I might also be deceitful and dishonest—and that dishonesty had become a way of life for me.

"I know now that my drug and alcohol use was an avoidance technique to escape my personal misery, and I was so distraught about DeeDee that I checked myself into a rehab clinic. Although I didn't want to hear anything about it, they taught me meditation.

"Learning to meditate has been amazing. It was so difficult to sit still, to quiet my thoughts and stop all the self-blame and negative internal conversations I'd been having with myself for years. Although the Yoga instructor wasn't a Buddhist or anything, he gave me a mantra, a foreign-sounding word that didn't mean anything to me. He said it was just a word, something that I was to say to myself over and over again. The purpose is that the sound begins to vibrate in your head and soon there isn't any room in there for any outside thoughts. I've struggled with the meditation and the mantra, and I believe I've managed to make some progress.

"While I was there, I also learned from a Yoga instructor about chakras and auras. I took all the quizzes and realized that not only did I have to work on my complete aura, I had to work on my throat chakra most of all. The rehab center, and particularly that one instructor, helped me get a good look at how self-deluding I have been.

"I've been out for almost a year now, and I haven't gone back to my old radio job. I got a regular 9 to 5 job, working in an advertising agency with one of the accounts that I had done commercials for when I was on the radio. They know all about me. There are no secrets about my substance abuse history. It feels so good to try to be honest and truthful with myself, my friends, and the people I work with.

"I'd like to say that I got back together with DeeDee, but that would have been like an ending in a romance novel and it didn't happen. However, I've met someone really nice in a New Age bookstore. Her name is Evelyn and she tells me she can see auras. I have to believe she can because the minute I began to tell even one little white lie, she says she can see my aura get darker and smaller. I'm working on being conscious of where and what I need to change and visualizing a bright shiny aura enveloping me. I think it is working because my future with Evelyn is looking very good."

Throat Chakra Tasks

Talk to a plant. Tell it how beautiful it is.
Name the most beautiful place on earth and go there, mentally.
If you had to tell your parents one of your secrets, what would it be?
Sing in the car on your way to work.
Listen to a recording artist who is unfamiliar to you.

Visualization

The color associated with the throat chakra is blue. Close your eyes and see the vibrations and sounds of the music of the distant planets coming toward you from the bright blue sky above. Visualize yourself creating new ideas as you listen, write, or participate in any form of the arts that communicates with others. See yourself speaking dynamically and authoritatively to a large group of enthusiastic people. Observe the energy of the throat chakra whirling around your neck, bringing with it an awareness of the deeper and subtle harmonics hidden in the vibrations of others' auras. See this energy strengthen and nourish all your relationships as you are nourished by them.

Meditation and Affirmation

Whatever you need, you can ask for. Positive thoughts create positive energy. You can ask the universe for whatever you need because it has an infinite power to create. As your life changes and grows, as you change and improve, as new people enter your circle of friends, you can alter and renew your meditation and your affirmation to suit the moment.

Throat Chakra Meditation

"As I breathe in, I inhale the good vibrations of the universe.
I exhale and leave behind me all the negative words that no
    longer affect my life.
I am connected to the music of the spheres.
I speak creatively and what I communicate removes
    boundaries."

Affirmation

"I choose to live a life where I am free to speak for myself."
"I accept that there are no mistakes in life, only lessons to be
    learned."

Throat Chakra Future

As you learn to speak from your heart and hear your words, your honesty will be appreciated and speaking your thoughts out loud will now cause you to soften them. You will find places to speak kindly that you hadn't thought of before and as you do, the ability to express your feelings will bring new life to old relationships. Wait and watch. Soon you will hear new beautiful sounds.

10 Heal Your Ability to See the World Around You

Every human has intuition and wise are they who
obey its signals. If it does not always tell us what
to do, it always cautions us what not to do.

—Wainetta Coffman
Teacher of meditation

In philosophy, intuition is a form of knowledge or thought that
is independent of experience or reason. The concept of intuition
was very important in ancient Greek philosophy. Scholars such as
Pythagoras, a trained mathematician, believed it to be basic to
any creative thought. It was also considered important in much of
Christian philosophy, as one of the basic ways to know God.
Baruch Spinoza believed it to be the highest form of knowledge;
Emmanuel Kant viewed it as the portion of perception that is sup-
plied by the mind itself; and Henri Bergson regarded it as the
purest form of instinct.

Perceive

The third eye chakra provides the energy to "see" beyond our five
senses. The Hindus call this third eye or brow chakra *ajna*, a word
that originally meant "to perceive." Through it, you can receive information beyond that provided from all of your other senses, and
you can greatly increase your ability to analyze the information you

receive every day, because it brings added understanding about the world and people around you.

Today, we often speak of such knowledge as having a hunch, getting a funny feeling, feeling it in one's bones, or getting an impression, and just as often we ignore, brush aside, or otherwise discount the information that this very real and protective third eye is trying to give us. It is the rare person who has not said, "I just knew there was something wrong," or "I should have paid more attention," or "The hair stood up on the back of my neck." Whether it is a new coworker, an introduction by a friend to someone who might be interesting to you, the casual meeting of a stranger in a public place, you would be very unusual if you have not said, "I knew right from the beginning that I shouldn't get involved because _____." (You fill in the blank.) As many of us know from bitter experience, if you had paid attention to those little nuances and clues, which are actually survival signals that tell you of the hidden danger in a seemingly harmless and smiling new acquaintance, you could have avoided a whole lot of trouble, heartache, and pain.

Beatrice

Beatrice, a senior at a prestigious university, had been to lots of campus parties and functions during her four years there and didn't consider any of the people she had met to be particularly dangerous. She said, "Some students are a little strange perhaps, but dangerous? No. I know that intuition is really is our danger radar, if we will only pay attention to it. I met this really charming guy at a party given by a group of divinity students, of all things. They all lived together in a large house and they all seemed to be serious and dedicated students. This charming guy and I sat together and talked for about an hour and then someone I knew came over and joined our conversation, and he moved on. At the end of the evening he offered to walk me to my off-campus apartment, which wasn't very far away. I found a couple of girls I knew who were ready to leave, too, so the three of us left together. He was sweet and appeared very shy and while I was attracted to him, there was just something about him that told me that I shouldn't be alone with him. I remember we all laughed at how disappointed he seemed when we waved good-bye to him. At the end of the semester, just before graduation, he was brought up on date rape charges by three different women. I am very grateful that I paid attention to my intuitive feeling about him. It possibly saved my life that night."

Seeing Beyond Your Other Senses

The sixth chakra or third eye, located in the center of the forehead, is considered the thinking chakra, the location of your ability to think creatively and understand the material and physical world. This chakra is different from all the previous five because it is said to be located within the brain. Its function is "seeing," although not in the sense that we see with our two eyes but in the ability to interpret the physical world as well as that of the astral plane. It is also the site of your intuitive self, the self-protective mechanism that tells you that things are different from whatever your other senses are telling you. Those with finely honed intuitive senses are often very sensitive to the auras of others and are able to avoid many problems by simply being quickly aware that people may be very different than the persona they attempt to present to the world.

A blocked or weak sixth attracts those people who are able to confuse you and create havoc with your ability to solve problems, and because so little energy can enter through a blocked sixth chakra, creative thinking and problem solving can be extremely limited. A strong sixth brings the ability to be creative, to find workable solutions to problems, to avoid procrastination, and to generate powerful productive thought processes. An energetic third eye will help you carry out your plans and ideas in a more practical manner, as well as visualize and understand concepts that previously were confusing. It will increase your ability to see to the core of others' ideas and avoid the pitfalls that often come with misunderstanding their behavior.

All life experiences, both positive and negative, are recorded and stored in the universe's energy system. It is one of the third eye chakra's tasks to tap into the resonating vibrations that every act of each person creates and to provide that information to you to help move your life to a higher level of functioning.

Although mystics say intuition is the whispering of angels, psychics claim it is some mysterious power that only they can access, and our grandmothers say it is just using plain old common sense, it is something we can all contact. Most of us have experienced a gut instinct, a sudden knowledge of the truth about something, or a feeling that appears to go against known facts that, in retrospect, has proved to be accurate. Often we brushed such thoughts aside rather than allowing ourselves to be guided by them.

It may be that those individuals who claim they are psychic have a fully functioning third eye chakra and receive informational patterns operating on an infinite number of invisible frequencies. "Perhaps they are just more finely tuned into the cosmos than the rest of us because it's not magic," says author of *The Intuitive Edge,* Philip Goldberg. "Intuition works with information that is not consciously available, that may have been stored in the past or acquired subliminally." It is that subliminally acquired information that you want to become more attuned to.

Hillary Wilson, an intuition trainer who gives seminars to professional groups, says, "Intuition will always take you in the right direction. I always tell my students, 'If you have doubts, don't.' You just have to quiet your busy intellect so that the third eye can see where you should go and what you should do. However, you can't just will intuition to happen. There are ways you can encourage it."

Rate Your Intuition

Answer the following to test your use of your sixth chakra:

1. Do you like to be left alone to decide how to proceed when given a problem to solve? Yes___ No___

2. If given help, would you rather the partner in the project be creative and imaginative?   Yes___ No___
3. Do you admire artistic and creative people, even if they are sometimes unreliable?   Yes___ No___
4. Do you prefer emotional friends over serious ones? Yes___ No___
5. Do you dislike routine?   Yes___ No___
6. Do you think you are a math klutz?   Yes___ No___
7. Do you like to sidestep the rules?   Yes___ No___
8. Do you frequently daydream during the day when you should be working?   Yes___ No___
9. If you have to put something together, do you prefer a picture to written instructions?   Yes___ No___
10. Do disorganized people annoy you?   Yes___ No___
11. Do you find emergencies to be exciting challenges? Yes___ No___
12. Do you find reading poetry pleasurable?   Yes___ No___
13. Do you observe people closely, looking for behavioral details, during conversation?   Yes___ No___
14. Do you often close your eyes when listening to music? Yes___ No___

If you have ten or more "yes" answers, you are already using your intuitive skills and your brow chakra well. If you had ten or more "no" answers, you might want to work to get your third eye operating with more power to help you be a better problem solver.

Fine-Tune Your Intuitive Skills

When you think rationally, reason logically, perform problem solving, and carry out the routine tasks of the day, your brain is operating in what is known as *beta* frequency, and unfortunately, that can contribute to the diminished powers of your third eye chakra. In order to help your third eye function, your brain needs to be operating in *alpha*. Actually, this is fairly simple to do because it happens every time you close your eyes. Then your brain generates a rapid burst of alpha waves and if you keep your eyes closed and relax, you will generate longer sustained periods of alpha. Studies have shown that it possible to control the wave activity of your brain, that you can learn to lower its operating frequency and to stop it from its habitual busy work by teaching yourself to relax on command and to visualize.

With practice, intuitive skills will improve and the answers you are looking for can come easily, from the energy of the universe.

1. Practice relaxation and meditation.

2. Keep a journal of your hunches and record what happened when you followed them or pushed them out of your mind.

3. Pay attention when you are performing some repetitive, "mindless" chore, such as sorting laundry or putting away the dishes. This is when your intellect is lulled and you can tune in to your intuitive insights.

4. Review first impressions. Does it feel right? Was there something that troubled you about the situation or the person? Visualize a big white movie screen in front of your third eye and then roll the film. You may be amazed by what you see.

5. Keep a dream journal. Ninety percent of intuitive messages occur in dreams.

6. Visualize (daydream) about goals you want to achieve.

7. Identify your intuitive response. Is it a vague feeling? A headache? The hair stands up on the back of your neck? A feeling in the pit of your stomach?

Create a Third Eye Chakra Environment

In order to be able to connect with your intuitive powers, the chakra in the center of the forehead must be strong and activated. The more practices you do that help you be calm, centered, and intent on bringing good into your life, the stronger this chakra will grow. As the third eye chakra becomes focused, you will transmit to others an aura of power, strength, wholeness, and stability. This chakra can become a strong defender against controllers, impostors, showoffs, tyrants, perfectionists, wet blankets, hypocrites, and all those people you never want in your life again.

Create a spot in your home where you can be quiet and relaxed. It can be a corner of your bedroom with a comfortable chair, a picture of a place you love, such as a mountain top or a lake, or even a religious object that gives you comfort and provides some serenity.

Meditation Brings Serenity

Transcendental Meditation, or TM, was brought to the West thirty-five years ago by Maharishi Mahesh Yogi. The Maharishi gave each person his or her own personal mantra (a sacred verbal formula, a word or a phrase, a syllable or portion of scripture containing mystical potentialities, which was repeated over and over by the meditator).

The Maharishi did meditation a great favor because he made it mainstream and provoked interest in it from people who were not particularly spiritual or religious. TM's popularity made serious study of the effects of meditation possible for the first time. In the last twenty years, more than five hundred studies have been made of its students by such leading research universities as Stanford, Harvard, and M.I.T. In these studies EEG measurement of the brain waves of the meditators indicated that they were producing a greatly increased amount of alpha waves (those brain waves that indicate a relaxed condition of the mind). Oxygen intake increased by approximately 18 percent while heart rates decreased by 25 percent and blood pressure was lowered. These effects are similar to that of deep rest, deeper than that of sleep, allowing for a greater alertness. The meditators reported a general feeling of relaxation, inner peace, and increased well-being, as well as improved academic performance, increased job satisfaction, and productivity. They further reported a decrease in the need for mind-altering substances (both prescription and recreational) and an increase in reaction times.

Corporations that included meditation training as part of their health-care package have found that employees who participated regularly got along better with peers and supervisors, missed less time due to illness, and ultimately found that the benefits of meditation pervaded their entire lives. Lorainne is a branch manager with a large bank, which has provided such training, she reported, "I find more value in my interpersonal relationships and generally feel more fulfilled as a person. All because I learned to meditate."

Techniques

People in many cultures meditate regularly and it is unfortunate that a frenetic modern society either looks upon meditation as something esoteric or just another time-consuming chore in an already busy life. According to the dictionary definition, meditation means ponder, reflect, or muse. There are as many differing techniques for meditation as the mind can create. In addition to repeating a phrase, a prayer, or a mantra, one of the most common is to focus on your own breathing. Many people visualize colors and shapes, or gaze with softened focus at some object, such as a candle flame, a crystal, or a flower. You needn't involve any religion or prayer in these moments, unless that is something that you are comfortable with.

There are an infinite variety of books, tapes and teachers of meditation and most of them suggest that you relax in a quiet, comfortable environment with clothing that is not too binding, where you will be neither too hot nor too cold. It is best to sit comfortably with the spine straight, which allows for the natural alignment of all the chakras and better transmission of energy up and down the connecting channel. A comfortable upright position is relaxing yet not so comfortable that you will go to sleep. Allow yourself a few moments to quiet your thoughts. Once you are comfortable, you can focus on your breathing, mentally repeat your affirmation or mantra, or gaze at something, such as the traditional candle flame. The purpose is to attempt to focus your mind on one thing only, in order to stop the mental static—that constant dialogue with yourself that is going on in your head—a definite roadblock to accessing your intuition.

Whatever the method or focus you select, repetition and concentration make meditation a discipline and a practice. As with any other activity that is practiced often, it becomes easier and more beneficial with time. To be of value, this brief time of meditation should soothe, relax, and make you feel calm, for that is its purpose.

Removing the "I Shouldn't Haves"

Our minds are always churning, thinking, regretting, tormenting us with "I shouldn't haves." These toxic thoughts do more than distract you. They are destructive to self-esteem, are rarely based on reality, and are seriously ego-damaging. If you have had some bad relationships (and who hasn't?), know that the "I shouldn't haves" are paralyzing. This busy mental activity keeps you locked into using your intellect, focused on the past, and prevents the generation of third eye chakra creative and intuitive energy. This constant thinking about and rehashing of problems and difficulties is detrimental because it seriously blocks your third eye chakra, with the result that it keeps your aura narrow and constricted.

1. Pick out one thing in your last relationship that you regret having done or said. (Example: You lost your temper.) Now go from that global concept (losing your temper) to the specifics of your behavior (you cursed and yelled).

2. Do not replay the entire scene in your head, but visualize yourself walking away from that situation with your head

held high and your dignity intact—before you lost your temper.

3. Using the specific behavior from number 1, grant yourself the power to know that you do not choose to behave that way again.

4. Pick out a specific behavior that harmed no one but yourself. (Example: I shouldn't have: eaten that/bought that/gone there.)

5. Create an affirmation for the future. Repeat this ego-boosting mantra to yourself several times. (Example: I am powerful and in control of my anger. I do not need to display it.)

Plan a Party

Plan a party. You have unlimited resources and can invite anyone, living or dead. List five people, male or female, you would invite.

———————   ———————   ———————   ———————   ———————

For each guest, state two traits you believe they possess as reasons to invite that person.

———————   ———————   ———————   ———————   ———————

———————   ———————   ———————   ———————   ———————

Look at the descriptive words you used about yourself in chapter 7 when you wrote your affirmation in the New Friend Quiz. Do any of these words now appear on your list of reasons for inviting your party guests? (Example: If you wrote "amiable" in your affirmation as a trait you thought others believed you to be lacking, and it appears as one of the reasons for inviting a guest, you can be reasonably certain that you are filling in a deficit you believe you have with your imaginary guest's skills. This knowledge will increase self-awareness, increase your ability to think creatively, and help balance and strengthen the aura of your sixth chakra.)

Observation Skills Test

The ability to observe will not only strengthen your third eye chakra but will help you in your ability to see people as they really are and keep you from involving yourself with potentially poor choices in a significant other. Mr. or Ms. Right may seem to have suddenly appeared before your very eyes, but by being a wary and attentive observer you may avoid those con artists and cheats who, unfortunately, are out there, looking for someone with a weak third eye chakra.

Without looking:

1. You have handled thousands of pennies in your life. Describe a penny.

2. Mentally go room by room through your house. How many light switches are there?

3. Describe the carpeting in one room in your house, including color, pile, stains, furniture indentations.

4. Describe in detail what your boss was wearing today, including shoes.

5. When you leave your house to go to work daily, you stop at the first red light. Describe what exists on all four corners of that intersection.

6. Pick any four states, including the one you live in. Write the symbol that appears on those license plates.

7. Recall the last time you ate out; could you pick out in a line up the waiter or waitress who served you?   Yes__   No__

8. Describe the chair or sofa you are sitting on. Did you include sounds, texture, the legs and feet, the odors?   Yes__   No__

If you are surprised that you didn't do as well on this test as you thought you should have, it is time to work on honing your powers of observation. The next time a potential love interest comes into view, the ability to look very carefully, size him or her up correctly, and intuitively recognize those little tiny clues that you might have overlooked before you strengthened your third eye chakra may save you a great deal of heartache.

Observation Skills Task

1. At the grocery store, look into a stranger's cart and then look away. How many items can you recall?

2. Watch a TV program with the sound off. Try reading both the body language and the lips of the performers.

3. Look out of your window at night after dark. Observe the shapes and outlines of things you see every day, such as the trees or the neighbor's air conditioner.

4. Take a walk around the mall. Look at couples; see if you can decide who is in charge in the relationship.

5. Listen to a sound outside your home. Without looking, identify and describe it.

6. Put into words the sound your front door makes when you close it, the sounds of the lock when the key turns in it.

7. When you hear a dog barking, describe what kind of a dog you think it is.

8. Listen to music and see if you can pick out individual instruments.

9. Describe the odor of the furnace the first time it is turned on after the summer.

10. Describe the smell of chlorine in a swimming pool.

11. Describe the aroma of your favorite flower.

12. Describe the fragrance of warm laundry when it comes out of the dryer.

Keep a Dream Journal

When you are sleeping, you generate *alpha, delta,* and *theta* brain waves, which are most beneficial to accessing your intuition. Keep writing materials or a small tape recorder beside your bed. Make your bedroom a relaxing peaceful place. Just before you go to sleep, tell yourself you are going to dream and when you wake up, write down or record whatever fragments of the dream you can recall. With a little practice you will find that you are dreaming frequently. Most of us dream all the time, we are just out of the habit of remembering what we dreamed.

You may be surprised; often the answers you are looking for are there when you wake up—a message from the universe telling you what to do.

Liz

Liz, a young designer with a firm that specializes in mid-priced women's fashions, was so busy that she hardly had time to keep her apartment clean or do any grocery shopping. She was always running out of juice or laundry detergent and would often just stop at some fast food place on the way home to pick up something.

"You'd think I would be too busy to even think about a relationship but, unfortunately, that hasn't been true. I really consider myself something that lots of my friends would laugh at now, but that is a 'woman who needs a man' and in this day and age, with women's lib and sexual harassment suits, I have trouble admitting that I am that kind of a woman. In the work that I do, I seldom see any men; it's all women and gorgeous models."

Liz rolled her eyes heavenward. "I know I have made a lot of mistakes about men, but then, who hasn't? My mother is having a fit over the way I meet somebody, and I decide they are okay and jump feet first into a relationship and, of course, later she gets to tell me, 'I told you so.' My whole family worries. My aunts, my uncles, my grandparents. They are all afraid of strangers and they are always warning me about how dangerous it is out there today. That's a great help to somebody like me, who jumps first and thinks about it later.

"I almost hesitate now to tell anybody about Pasquale, but my friends and family would have called the men in the white coats to come and take me away if they had known about him at the time. I met him in a pizza shop. He wasn't making pizzas; he was a customer. He was soooo handsome, he had big brown eyes and a great shock of unruly black hair. I have to admit it, there was just raw sexual energy between us immediately. I left with him, a pizza, and a bottle of red wine, and we went back to his place. Twenty-four hours later I was on a plane to Italy with him! I never even called my employer at the time to tell him I wasn't coming in. We had a wonderful time for two months, until the limit on my credit card was exhausted. Naturally, I found out that he had a wife and a couple of kids someplace in northern Italy and I guess I'm lucky that by that time we were so worn out that I could see it was time for me to come home.

"Then there is Daveed Maganeese, a lawyer. He is tall with a reddish tint to his hair and beard, and very, very handsome. I met him in Mexico when I went there for a short vacation. We had a whirlwind romance, and I guess I fell in love with his image. He claimed that he was an international lawyer, dealing with the cruise ship industry. His Spanish was so beautiful. I didn't always know what he was saying to me, but it sounded so romantic that I just turned to Jell-O when he gazed into my eyes and sang to me in Spanish. When I went back home, he wrote to me and I almost fainted when I saw the name on the return address. It was David Maginus and he is Irish, from Chicago. He's not Mexican at all! I didn't even have to learn the rest of story; that name finished it for me. It sounded so lyrical, so poetic with the Spanish pronunciation and so ordinary with the American one. Of course, it turned out that he was a steward on a cruise ship, not a lawyer, and probably he wasn't even speaking Spanish to me most of the time. I just thought he was.

"For a while I talked about my adventures and how I was living like a lot of other people just wish they could, but don't have the nerve to take risks. Now, I'm beginning to have a lot of regrets and realize just how foolish I have been and how dangerous some of these 'adventures' could have turned out to be." Liz thought for a moment. "I guess I'm lucky to be alive but I still have to pause and get a grip when I meet a new man and realize that they often aren't who they say they are, even though I always want to believe them.

"I'm really working on my observational skills. I've gone back over some of the relationships I've had, not just with Pasquale and Daveed, and I now know that there were lots of little clues that I could have tuned in to and saved myself a lot of heartache and disappointment. I've got to stop feeling so lonely, and so desperate, and love starved that I take up with just anybody. I've started keeping a dream journal and I have been amazed at what it has taught me, not only about the men I meet but about my job and my relationships with my family. My mother has spent a lot of hours worrying about me. She says I have no internal radar and I guess she has been right. I think I'm beginning to grow up now and I've been working on tuning up my intuitive skills. I know I have some because they work wonderfully when it comes to fabric and design, so I guess I can use that as a clue to help me be more intuitive about the men I meet. And also," Liz laughed, "I guess I have to spend more than a few hours with a guy before I decide he's the one for me."

Richard

Richard kept his eyes down and his hands in his pockets. He said, "I know how people describe me; even my mother says I'm 'painfully shy.' I've been called timid and bashful, too. I guess those are accurate descriptions. I design Web pages for many companies who are getting on the Internet and I spend a lot of hours alone, staring at a computer, deciding how to make someone's product leap off the screen. The worst part of my job is talking to the customers, learning about what they sell, and making presentations of what I have created for them, like a salesman with a product.

"I guess when it comes to meeting women, I am shy. I really don't think I have the kind of small talk skills a lot of guys my age have. I don't know why that is. I guess it's because I'm just a computer geek at heart. What usually happens is that women begin talking to me, mostly at work because they have to deal with me on some project or another. Several of them have said they liked me because I was so intelligent and humble at the same time, whatever that means. I've never asked a girl to go anyplace. I've never learned to dance. I don't play any sports because I'm not very coordinated. Now, because I'm thirty, my mother is worried that I'll never get married. I do date occasionally because some girl asked me over for a home-cooked meal or wanted advice on buying a computer so she could get into some chat rooms, but it's never been a big deal for me.

"Lately I started to procrastinate a lot at work and that has me more worried than thinking about whether or not I'll ever get married. I seemed to have the equivalent of writer's block. We did a Web page for a company that sells cameras, and they have one that they claim will actually photograph human auras. That is what got me interested in the subject because I had to understand all about these cameras to create a Web page. The information about the third eye chakra and creativity seemed to be directed right at me because I have been having real trouble with grasping some concepts I need to understand. I've been practicing my observational skills and," Richard pushed his glasses up on the bridge of his nose, "those observational skills have suddenly made me notice Mary, a girl at work. I've seen her around for several years but now there seems to be things about her I'm noticing that I like." He smiled shyly. "Maybe I'll ask Mary out."

Third Eye Chakra Tasks

Wear something purple—earrings or socks.

Close your eyes; hear a bird song in your head.

What is the last mistake you made? What is the lesson you
learned?

Pick a cause that interests you. Decide to stand up for it.

Take a walk and go as far as you can see. When you get there,
notice what you can see farther on that road.

Did you learn something new today? What was it?

Remind yourself: Today is here. Did you use it well?

Visualization

Visible color is produced by variations in the wavelengths of light.
The hot colors, such as red and orange, are of a lower frequency
than the cool colors, such as blue and violet.

The color associated with the third eye chakra is purple. This
"seeing" chakra is associated with the phenomenon of light and
the absence of light—darkness. Ultraviolet radiation, radio waves,
X-rays, and microwaves are just of a few of the many vibrations
within this spectrum of light that are not visible to the human eye.
The ability to "see" things that are hidden or dark is intensified by
focusing on your third eye chakra.

Visualize that you can see in the dark with the clarity of a cat.
Close your eyes and imagine your third eye chakra, which is located in the center of your forehead, glowing brightly. Imagine that
someone looking at you would see this bright light, which changes
to include colors from the palest violet through indigo to the deepest shade of purple. Bring in more light from the universe to enter
through your third eye and cast glowing energy on the darkest corners of your thoughts, your gloomiest hours, your saddest life
experiences. Visualize your third eye glowing brighter, filled with
intuitive energy that will increase your creativity and bring strength
to your ability to see your life and your future with reality, shining
with hope.

Meditation and Affirmation

Whatever it is that you need, see it with clarity coming into your future. Plan that your life will be good, that your feet will take you on the path you wish, and that on that path you will meet the people you need. Life is always about choices. Plan to make good ones.

Meditation

"As I breathe in, I bring clarity and wisdom to my vision.
As I breathe out, I leave behind me all that I no longer need to see.
I am deeply connected to the power of the universe.
My vision is clear and I look forward to the future with joy."

Affirmation

"I choose a life with joyous and creative new ideas in sight."
"I choose to meet a lover who is intuitive and sensitive to my needs."

Third Eye Chakra Future

As you become more intuitive, you will begin to see the people in your life with greater clarity. Perhaps some will dim in your view and some you hadn't noticed before will begin to glow with a new light. Look around you. Perhaps you will see something you want.

11 Heal Your Connection With the Cosmos

> Every man takes the limits of his own field
> of vision for the limits of the world.
>
> —Arthur Schopenhauer

The crown chakra provides the energy for you to reach for enlightenment and spirituality in order to connect with cosmic consciousness. The crown chakra, which is located at the top of the head, helps you to integrate your total being and experience a connection with the cosmos through your unique spirituality. It is your direct connection with your spiritual life, the realm of higher consciousness. Too often in our busy lives, any connection with higher consciousness, spirituality, or the contemplation of personal moral values or consideration of ethical dilemmas is reserved for an occasional thought about religion or how we wish others would behave. Perhaps you go to church on special holidays or say Grace before a meal. Often, your thoughts about injustice or morality are the result of feeling that someone has harmed or angered you and most of us have called on God or some higher power, something or someone greater than ourselves, in a time of emergency or need.

It really doesn't matter if you have prayed or spoken words of hope and longing or gratitude to the Goddess, the Universe, the Holy Spirit, Allah, Brahma, Amen Ra, Jehovah, Ancestors, or a Guardian Angel. What matters is that at some time, you prayed or spoke to something or someone larger, more glorious, something or someone inspirational, who exists outside of yourself, a beginning step toward a personal experience that can transcend mere self-interest.

The Crown Chakra

Hindus believe that the seventh or crown chakra is the foundation upon which enlightenment can begin. It is the center and origin of consciousness. They believe that becoming conscious, or enlightened, is an experience beyond reason, beyond all the senses and beyond the limits of the known world all around us. They see reaching such a state as the ultimate in "knowing." Called *nirvana* in Buddhism, it is the ideal condition of harmony, stability, and joy, a personal connection to a higher power that brings eternal bliss.

Other religions, though they don't speak of chakras, all acknowledge that there is a personal connection to a higher power that can deliver every individual from the destructive forces of evil. Whether it is reached through good works, good prayer, good living, or all three, they believe that this ecstasy of salvation can result in a state of spiritual joy.

A weak seventh chakra brings those people into your life who are able to disturb your peace of mind and create confusion in you about your beliefs, your purpose, and your goals. A strong seventh will repel those individuals who would lead you astray from your noble and inspirational goals and dreams. A crown chakra that is open to that connection to the cosmos will bring comfort and peace and a stable belief system of some kind, whether it is solely personal or organized, one that will guide your actions and provide you with the firm knowledge that you are secure in your place in the order of things. Opening the crown chakra will manifest the ability to reach into the infinite for new thought and new ways of knowing and feeling. Your belief system will be strengthened and you will become aware of your ability to learn and grow, to see the divine spark that has given you a life to be lived with integrity.

Michelangelo

Between 1508 and 1512, Michelangelo created the frescoes on the ceiling of the Sistine Chapel, one of the glories of the Vatican in Rome. On that ceiling he depicted nine scenes from Genesis, the first book of the Old Testament. These luminous pictorial images represented the stages of creation—beginning with the creation of the cosmos, where God separated the earth from the waters, created the sun, the moon, and the planets, and separated light from darkness with a mighty primordial force. In the scene where God creates Adam, the first man is unable to act until the touch of God's fingers endows him with a soul. That spark of humanity, passing from God to man, was depicted by this famous artist as a moment equal to the creation of the cosmos, requiring a glorious transfer of energy.

Now, in the 1990s, man has launched the Hubble Space Telescope, which is bringing back much information about the beginnings of our universe. Staring down to corridor of the southern sky, it has looked 12 billion light-years away and spied a multitude of thousands of never-before-seen galaxies, colliding and merging. While scientists expect that it will answer some of the questions about how the world began, and perhaps even why, the information it is bringing back about the energy in the vast cosmos has awed and stunned serious students of both astronomy and religion.

The energy of the cosmos, flowing through, in, and out of the chakras, creating an aura that is visible to some and felt by all, of a flowing, interactive, electrodynamic energy field, should be readily understood and accepted as a very small part of our universe by anyone who can recognize the dynamic creation of the cosmos—as seen by an artist hundreds of years ago, who showed it to us with the inspired work of his hands on a chapel ceiling, and the inspired work of thousands of scientists who originated the Hubble, which brings us the amazing reports about what has happened and what is happening out there in the starry night.

Values and Traditions

We are living in a time of intense social change, and many people have moved away from organized religion. As a result, it appears that "There is definitely a spiritual hunger in the world today. There is an awakening worldwide of the need for some of the values and traditions that our parents had, the kinds of spiritual messages and inspirational thoughts we may have heard as children and that many of us seem to have lost somewhere along the way," according to non-denominational minister Donald Wood. This spiritual hunger has led people down different paths, to traditional churches and synagogues, and to Eastern philosophies and offshoots of all of the conventional theologies. "What matters," says the Rev. Wood, "is that people are seeking answers, looking for peace of mind and significant rules to govern their lives."

For two thousand years the Ten Commandments, plus the Golden Rule, the precept that people should do to others as they would have others do to them, have served as proverbial guidelines of conduct, models by which to live, for Christians, Jews, and others.

The ten rules for living, according to the Old Testament, were given by Jehovah to Moses on Mount Sinai, inscribed on two stone tablets. Two different versions of the commandments are given in Exodus 20:1–17 and Deuteronomy 5:6–21, but the substance is the same in both.

Most Protestants and Orthodox Christians combine some of them but ultimately, they are the same. In the Jewish tradition, they are as follows:

1. Prologue, declaring that this is the word of God
2. Prohibition against the worship of any deity but Jehovah, and the prohibition against idolatry
3. Prohibition against using God's name in vain
4. Observance of the Sabbath
5. Honoring one's parents
6. Prohibition against murder

7. Prohibition against adultery
8. Prohibition against stealing
9. Prohibition against giving false testimony
10. Prohibition against coveting a neighbor's property or wife

As we examine these ten rules for living, any serious analysis of their meaning will bring the realization it might be a good idea to:

Avoid idolizing things like money, power, success, and possessions.
Acknowledge a power greater than yourself through good words and deeds.
Keep your obligations and commitments.
Treat others with kindness and justice.
Avoid humiliating behavior that can kill your soul.
Respect other people's property and reputation.
Avoid wanting what others have.

For an even longer period of time, another major world religion, Buddhism, has suggested that believers follow the Eightfold Path, which consists of:

Right views
Right intention
Right speech
Right action
Right livelihood
Right effort
Right-mindedness
Right contemplation

Examine Your Ethics

If you've been disappointed time and time again by a partner who is angry, unreliable, jobless, selfish, overly dramatic, immature or controlling, dishonest, a cheat, a liar, a coward, a bully—whose behavior often left you disappointed, hurt, angry, and regretful and who has left you confused and worried about where the relationship might lead, answer the following:

1. Have you ever taken something small from your employer? (Example: box of paper clips, tape to wrap Christmas presents.) Yes___ No___

2. Have you ever shoplifted? Yes___ No___ (Example: a small toy or a piece of fruit in the grocery store.)

3. Have you ever been so angry at someone you wished them harm? Yes___ No___

4. Have you ever told a lie or repeated gossip just to stir things up? Yes___ No___

5. Have you ever driven while intoxicated? Yes___ No___

6. Have you ever sworn at or indulged your frustration with another driver while traveling at a high rate of speed? Yes___ No___

7. Have you ever telephoned an old love late at night just to check up on whether they were home? Yes___ No___

8. Have you ever lied to a friend's husband or wife to cover for them? Yes___ No___

9. Have you accepted lying or chronic lateness from your significant other because you were afraid of losing that person if you didn't? Yes___ No___

8. Have you ever dated someone you weren't interested in just to make another person jealous? Yes___ No___

9. Have you ever told someone you loved him or her just because it was the easiest thing to do at the time? Yes___ No___

10. Have you ever cheated on an exam? Yes___ No___

11. Have you ever cried, pouted, thrown things, or slammed doors just to get your way, even when you knew you were wrong? Yes__ No__

12. Have you ever called your parents when you wanted something and pretended it was just to see how they are? Yes__ No__

13. Have you ever exaggerated a minor illness for sympathy? Yes__ No__

14. Have you ever dated someone you knew was married? Yes__ No__

15. Have you ever borrowed something, knowing you had no intention of returning it? Yes__ No__

In an informal survey of college students, a majority admitted to almost all of these behaviors and thought most of them were harmless, that they fell into the category of being no more than "little white lies."

Most of us have strong internal directives about what is right and what is wrong, learned during childhood from a variety of sources: parents, other relatives, friends, parents, school, church or synagogue, youth organizations, Sunday school, and peers. We often don't articulate our moral beliefs; we just know where we draw the line for our own behavior. Unfortunately, today there are many young people growing up without the stability of any of these resources to guide them and as a result they inflict pain upon others without ever considering the consequences of such behavior. Perhaps you were in a relationship with one of these individuals, whose behavior was less than desirable and you made excuses for this person because you didn't think a little exaggeration, a little white lie, was very important.

To every question to which you gave a "yes" response, list who was the victim. (Example: Question number 1—the employer's balance sheet.)

Now provide a justification for that behavior. (Example: I'm underpaid. Everyone does it. The bosses have millions.)

Reexamine those "yes" responses. Now list yourself as the victim.

Now give a reason. (Example: Question number 1—that makes me a thief.)

Which of those behaviors to which you answered "yes" would you find acceptable in a friend, companion, or significant other?

These answers should be used as a resource for examining the kind of partner or friends you are willing to accept into your life. It doesn't take much thought to see that if you are willing to make excuses for such behavior in yourself, others who are also willing to do the same will sense from your aura that you are accepting of someone whose moral boundaries may be fuzzy or even non-existent. Relationships with people who accept lying, cheating, and stealing have no place to go but downhill. Your thoughts about your answers will make ethical issues real and will strengthen the seventh chakra as unconscious behavior is brought to your consciousness.

A strong crown chakra will project a calm spirituality and will aid in repelling those who would lead you away from a principled life that brings joyous relationships.

A Life Grant

Most of us have tried to imagine what it would be like to win a huge lottery, to suddenly come into the possession of millions of dollars for the price of a single ticket. We could become fantastically wealthy overnight and never have to work again in our lives. Probably we all think that it would be wonderful. The sad statistics about what happens in the lives of lottery winners indicate that many of them end up unhappy, feel cut off from their friends and families, go bankrupt because of bad investments, or find themselves embroiled in lawsuits.

However, imagine that you were given a small grant. This grant, with no strings attached, would provide you with an additional income that would take you five years to earn. You could live in the manner you do now without having to work, if you so desired. The money would be yours to do with as you wish. At the end of the five years you would need to earn a living again and become responsible for your future. What would you do?

Select one:

1. Keep your present job and bank the money.
2. Leave your job and travel the world.
3. Go back to school and study: _____ (fill in the blank).
4. Get extensive plastic surgery and a new wardrobe.
5. Move to an artists' colony to: write, paint, sculpt, and so forth.
6. Donate it all to a worthy charity: medical research, homeless shelter, abused children, and so on.
7. Provide a college education for a deserving and talented person you know.
8. Throw a huge party and buy presents for everyone you know.
7. Make life more comfortable for your parents.
8. Invest it.
9. Go to Las Vegas and bet it all.
10. _____ (fill in the blank).
11. Buy a boat, plane, vacation home, and so forth.
12. Become a ski bum, a surfer, a scuba diver, and so on.

As you examine which of these you selected, it is easy to see that there is a difference between an altruistic and a self-interested choice. However, a self-interested choice is not necessarily selfish because by self-improvement you are contributing to the world around you, becoming more interesting, more desirable, and more humane. A number of the choices do not require you to change your present day-to-day world, only that you make different use of your free time. Write a brief paragraph that elaborates how the choice you made will change you.

_____

_____

_____

Goal-Setting

As you look ahead and think about how changing your aura will bring into your life people who are more caring, more loving, more sharing, and more trustworthy, it is time to give some thought to the future. As you change and your aura changes, you must prepare for the differences that will occur.

1. Set some goals for yourself.
   In one year from today I want to _____.
   In two years from now I want to _____.
   In three years from now I want to _____.
   In four years from now I want to _____.
   In five years from now I want to _____.

2. List two goals you have just expressed that you think would alter your ability to attract the kind of person you want in your life. (Example: lose weight, learn a foreign language.)

   _____   _____

3. Imagine that you could *travel* to any place in the world. Select two destinations. _____   _____
   Give two reasons why you want to visit these places.

   _____   _____

4. If you could *live* any place in the world, where would that be?
   _____ If that place is different from the ones you selected to visit briefly, list three reasons why.

   _____   _____   _____

5. If you could select one person to go with you, who would
   that be? _____
   Give one reason why. _____

6. If that one person could not go with you, what would you
   need to change to make traveling alone possible?

   _____

7. If you could live anywhere, would your life goals be different
   there than they are at present? If so, list them.

   _____   _____   _____

An examination of life goals against various or foreign backgrounds, where you are separated from everyone and everything
that you know and can rely on, can sometimes reveal their inappro-
priateness, or can be a breakthrough in seeing them as real possibilities instead of unattainable dreams. (Example: If you want to live in
Paris and you selected one person to go with you because they speak
the language, learning to speak French might become a necessity instead of something you might do sometime in the future.)

Examine the reason you gave for selecting the individual to go
with you. Think about whether you chose that person because
he or she would be protective, act as a buffer against the unknown,
or for some other reason that helped you avoid taking responsibility
for yourself. You have made progress if you chose that person because
he or she: is fun to be with; would be interested in the same things
as you; is someone you feel comfortable with in strange situations;
and is someone with whom you could spend large blocks of time.

Social Conscience

Hyde school in Bath, Maine, is a private boarding school. It has a
thirty-year-old program for forming values and developing the character of its students. Headmaster Malcolm Gauld feels it is important to give the students value-forming experiences. "They aren't
taught character. It is a part of every experience at the school, from
sporting events to the classroom. They are encouraged to develop

their potential in five key traits—courage, integrity, concern, curiosity, and leadership—through a system of rewards and punishments."

Recently, a number of other schools have begun operating under the Hyde principles because they believe it is necessary to work against a present-day culture that says do whatever you feel like doing, rather than do what is right.

Answer the following:

1. What is your reaction to someone on the corner holding a "will work for food" sign?
   Pity _____   Anger _____   Disdain _____   Compassion _____
   Do you:
   Look away _____   Give them money _____   Offer a job _____

2. A charitable organization calls asking for a donation of old clothing. Do you:
   Look through your closet _____   Tell them you have none _____

3. A film of starving children comes on your TV. Do you:
   Change the channel _____   Think it's probably a scam _____
   Write them a check _____

4. A discussion of politicians and ethics occurs. Do you:
   Say nothing _____   Have an opinion _____   Defend them _____

5. Do you vote?   Yes__   No__

6. Have you ever picketed for or against some cause?
   Yes__   No__

7. An ethnic or racial joke is told in a large group. Do you:
   Laugh _____   Object _____   Keep quiet _____

8. A married friend is having an affair. Do you:
   Mind your own business _____   Tell the spouse _____
   Let your friend think you approve _____   Disapprove vocally _____

9. A teenager you know is using drugs. Do you:
    Tell the parents _____ Call the cops _____ Mind your own
    business _____ Talk to the teen _____

Each individual situation is different. It is a matter of your
own judgment about the particular situation and your own values.
However, it is obvious that character counts because it is
the framework within which we all live. Character determines what
we do, how we make decisions, how we treat others, and how we
respond when the going gets tough. Decisions are made according
to your own values and those are revealed by character, which sets
the course of a life, all relationships, a family, and your future.

Brian

Brian said, "'My parents were very religious and as a child I resented it all: the prayers at the dinner table, reading the Bible,
memorizing stories for Sunday school, the endless hours spent
in church on my knees, and all the things I had to do as a child
that my parents saw as necessary for paving my way to heaven. I
wasn't very old when I rebelled against the strict religious rules that
were laid down by my parents and enforced with a very heavy
hand because there was nothing joyous about it. It was all about
sin and punishment. I couldn't wait to get out, swear, smoke,
drink, dance, stay out all night, listen to shock rock groups, and
do all the things that all the other teenagers I knew were doing
without giving a thought to their eternal soul. I couldn't see that
there was much wrong with most of those things and I realize now
that my family belonged to a very narrow, very strict church. My
friends called my parents 'Bible thumpers,' and nobody wanted to
come to my house because they would get a lecture and be asked
to kneel and pray on the front porch before they could come in. I
was always so embarrassed that I made excuses so I could meet
them elsewhere.

"I don't think I've ever really done anything that would be considered 'bad' by today's standards but by my parents' standards, I'm

well on my way to spending eternity in flames. I don't really have any goals except to relax and have a little fun. I've worked at several jobs since I graduated from high school and left my parent's house to live on my own. I've worked in a bakery, a hardware store, and I was even a trash collector for a while. Currently, I work in a grocery store, one that has a program to employ people with disabilities who bag the groceries, pick up the carts, and things like that. It was there that I met Maureen, one of the so-called disabled. The other employees call her Forrest Gump, you know, the movie character, because she has the same IQ as him, seventy-five. If Maureen is a little slow, it really doesn't matter to me, because she is the most wonderful, caring, kind human being I have ever known.

"My life has really changed since I met her and her family, and it is all for the better. Her parents are wonderful. Her father is a doctor and her mother a teacher and maybe that is what has given them such a wise understanding of her. They have been so good with Maureen. They have seen to it that she has been given every opportunity to become as much as she can be. They have mainstreamed her and never allowed people to make her feel bad about herself.

"They often say, 'Yes, she is a little slow, but we can take the time for her to understand and so should everyone else. There are so many wonderful things about Maureen that everybody should be glad to know her. We are happy she is our daughter. When she was first born, friends would ask us how we felt, knowing that our child would never become a doctor or a teacher. Sometimes they would have difficulty accepting that we like Maureen for the gift to us that she is. She has taught us patience and fortitude. She is so brave and willing and she tries to learn anything she is presented with, despite the odds.'"

Brian smiled as he thought about this family. "Her parents are so cheerful and happy and they all have such a good time together. It's great to spend time in their house. Her entire family says they can see auras and they talk about what they see and what it means very matter-of-factly. I'd never heard of auras before and when they described my aura to me and told me what the colors meant, I have to admit that they saw things about me that were true and things I thought and felt that I never told to a single soul."

Brian paused. "Maureen told me that she could see that my crown chakra was completely closed, and she was very worried about that because it meant that I didn't and couldn't have any peace of mind. At first I laughed about that, but the more I thought about it I realized that what she was saying was true. I have been brooding about my upbringing and dwelling on all kinds of negative thoughts about religion and death."

Brian's voice softened. "Maureen's parent's have made me feel like I am a member of their family. They are so supportive of Maureen and proud of her and her job; they make her feel as if she is special, and she is. She bought me a small quartz crystal, because that is the mineral associated with the crown chakra. I wear it on a chain around my neck during the day, and when I sit down to meditate I place it on my dresser so I can focus on it. When they first told me about meditation, I was really against it because I thought it was like all the prayers I had to say when I was a child, asking for forgiveness for my sins and all the bad stuff I supposedly had done. Maureen's mother explained to me that it was a little like daydreaming, just letting my thoughts wander. It took me a while, but now not only do I look forward to it, I enjoy it. I'm trying hard to understand my parents and my attitude toward them actually is softening. Maureen says she sees the color of my aura around the top of my head getting less and less muddy all the time."

Maureen

Maureen, at twenty-two, appears to be content with her job at the grocery store. She said, "I actually love my job. When I get to take the groceries to the car, I walk alongside the people and they smile and talk to me. I have met so many nice people that I look forward to going to work every day. I know that people think I am a little slow, and maybe I am.

"I also know that I have some special talents because I've been able to see people's auras all my life. When people ask me about it and I tell them my parents can see them, too, they are amazed because they didn't think a doctor or a teacher would see such things. In fact, I didn't know that other people didn't see them. I was surprised when I learned that. Seeing auras helps me a lot because I know which people I can talk to and which ones would rather just be left alone. The people at the store all like me, and I don't mind that sometimes they treat me like I am a child because I know that we are all God's children. My parents have taught me that spirituality is a sacred journey, an adventure that can be found in everyday life. I always think of that because you have to do everything with respect, as if you value the experience. Petting an animal, pruning a shrub, cleaning the house, answering a question from a little kid. All of these things need to be done carefully, respectfully, and I try to do that. Maybe that is one of the reasons people think I'm a little slow because I try to do all these things with what my teacher calls 'respectful regard.' "

Maureen looked at Brian and smiled. "I really love Brian. He has been so sad and so gloomy and since he is working on his aura he feels so much better. He is really a kind and generous person and I value him as my friend. We have talked about getting married, but my parents feel that we both need to know each other for a lot longer because there is a lot that Brian has to understand about me and how I am, and there is a lot I need to learn about Brian because I have been sheltered by my parents and have never really had a boyfriend before. I'm willing to wait because I know that Brian is a good person and if it is meant that we belong together, it will happen."

Change Your Focus, Change Your Future

When it comes to moral choices and the development of strength of character, it doesn't matter whether or not you had any formal religious upbringing. As you mature and grow, you may find your values change and those of any potential partner. Personal growth should be a reinforcement of your already existing spiritual strengths. As you change your focus, to making your life better you automatically change your future.

Someone very clever once said, "When Moses received the word of God on Mount Sinai and came down with the Ten Commandments, he wasn't bringing back the Ten Suggestions."

When you have all your chakras in line, they will spin with energy and communicate with each other up and down the channel beside your spinal column. Your aura will now expand and grow and you will experience an altered life. As change occurs, energy changes. These energy changes will cause your universe to expand and enlarge the energy flow that you desire and need.

Crown Chakra Tasks

Know that every thought has a consequence. What was your first thought this morning?

Say your affirmation for today out loud, as if it were a prayer.

Wear white.

Send a postcard to an old friend, just to say hello.

Go to a bookstore and look pictures in a book about the restoration of the Sistine Chapel.

Give a small gift to a homeless shelter.

Meditation and Visualization

Although the crown chakra is the last to be considered, your work on it should never be put off while you focus on the lower chakras because this chakra crowns the entire system. It is the beginning of enlightenment, beyond the physical world around you. Perhaps a meditation or a visualization will comfort and support you—and will also help you comprehend the order in the cosmos, through which comes a divine spark opening a gateway to greater understanding.

Understand that the universe is totally abundant. It contains everything your heart could ever desire, on the material, emotional, mental, and spiritual planes. All that you need and want is there for the asking. Believe in this abundance, desire it, and then be willing to accept it when the universe provides.

Meditation

"As I breathe in, I inhale a connection with a power greater
than myself.

As I exhale, I leave behind me all that prevents my creative
self-expression.

I am joined with a silver cord to the great power of the
cosmos.

I create a new life with new rules of behavior from Divine
guidance."

Visualization

Close your eyes and see a full moon above you, shining down
with crystal clear light on the crown of your head, pouring the energy of a power greater than yourself into your thoughts, giving
you integrity and moral and ethical strength.

Affirmation

"I choose to live a life where character counts."
"I choose to allow into my life a lover whose moral values I can
respect."

Crown Chakra Future

Think honorable thoughts,
Think just thoughts,
Think lovely thoughts,
Think gracious thoughts,
Think praiseworthy thoughts,
Think excellence and truth.

Watch carefully for powerful yet gentle changes—expect them.
Look and you will see it happen. Think and you will create what
you think you deserve.

12 Heal How You Hold On to Old Memories

> The memory is like a cat scratching at my heart.
>
> —Marina Oswald

By performing the tasks and exercises in the previous chapters, you have brought unconscious material up to your consciousness. You may have discovered that you have certain moral dilemmas that need to be resolved before you can move on. Perhaps you found that you repeatedly jump into relationships based on superficial things that makes a new person appear to be a lot of fun—but when the fun is over, there really isn't very much there. Perhaps you found some of these exercises more difficult than others and some of the thoughts they evoked proved painful, particularly if they made you examine how you repeated some of the same mistakes in previous relationships. The very act of bringing unconscious material up to your conscious mind, by becoming aware of how you respond to others, by examining and attempting to understand your physical, emotional, and spiritual life, you have automatically unblocked and energized your chakras and altered the aura that they manifest.

Two questions remain:

1. If you can't see your aura, how do you know that you have repaired it?
2. Are these changes to your chakras and your aura permanent?

Cellular Memory

Paul Pearsall, in his book *Heart's Code,* provides us with some well-researched facts about cellular memory. Although Pearsall is writing about the cells of the heart, he states that all of the cells of the body are made up of energy-conducting walls with various information receptors and a nucleus that serves as each and every cell's mini-brain. In addition, each cell of the body is 99.999 percent empty space. Subatomic bundles of energy whizz through this empty space at the speed of light.

Anesthesiologist Stuart Hameroff, a professor of Anesthesiology College of Medicine, University of Arizona Health Sciences Center in Tucson, Arizona, suggests that cells' micro-tubules are perfectly designed information-processing devices. He calls them "information-energetic computers." Hameroff believes that each person's cells are that individual's unique memory storage system.

Like a Bolt Out of the Blue

Scientists in the 1960s detected a biomagnetic field projected from the human heart, and in the early 1970s scientists at MIT, using SQUID magnetometers, confirmed these heart studies and went on to detect much smaller fields around the head. The Institute of HeartMath at Boulder Creek, California, made television news recently when it was reported they had scientifically documented what happens in the process of two people "falling in love." A couple sharing romantic candlelight dinners, a man impelled to send flowers and heart-shaped boxes of candy, a woman writing love notes and applying lipstick, can all be the result of a scientifically documented experience. When one individual is attracted to another, that person's heart actually sends electrical energy directly to the heart of the other, and if the attraction is mutual, that heart responds in kind. The Cupid's arrow into the heart that we have all seen on pretty Valentine's Day cards may actually be a flash of spinning electrons, which results in an instantaneous jolt, a shock of energy, directly between the hearts of lovers, resulting in that shower of sparks, the emotional fireworks we all call love.

Most of these scientists would probably be surprised to know that the things they are documenting were already understood by ancient philosophers who, although they didn't have scientific technical knowledge, understood that there were energy generators in the human body. They called them *chakras*. They understood that there was energy that was transmitted to the outside of each person's body. They called it an *aura*. Today's scientists are confirming, with sophisticated research and scientific documentation, what these philosophies have known and understood for centuries.

Love Can Be a Pain in the . . .

We have already suggested that memory is locked into the cells of your body. Specifically, memory is locked into the connective tissue of your body. Every part of your body—your bones, muscles, organs, blood vessels, and nerves—is surrounded and intermeshed with this semi-elastic fibrous material. This connective tissue, known as the fascia, is interwoven all throughout your body. The superficial fascia is a sheath just below your skin and it is directly connected to similar sheaths around each individual muscle and internal organ, even around the membrane of each and every cell, all 75 trillion of them.

The main ingredient of connective tissue is a protein known as collagen, which has the ability to change in texture from a gelatin-like substance to something much tougher and thicker. We have all seen a tiny baby easily put his toes into his mouth and if we could see into the future we would be amazed to see this same baby as an elderly man shuffling along, barely able to turn his head from side to the side, but if we could envision it, it would illustrate the extremes of the flexibility of connective tissue.

When anyone sustains an injury, whether it is physical or emotional, instinct provides us with a defensive response against the blow. We protect ourselves with tension. If the injury is repeated and we continue guarding against it, we will discover that, over time, our connective tissue in particular places has hardened to the consistency of tough, inflexible leather. This connective tissue, where memories are stored, can become permanently rigid as we tighten up our muscles to protect our feeling each hurt or injury.

Almost everyone has some spot where tension is locked in. There are very few of us who haven't felt at one time that a loved one was "a pain in the neck." Although you might not have connected that thought to a later occurrence, you may have awakened a few mornings later with a stiff neck. Perhaps you have wished that someone would "get off your back," and then shortly thereafter lifted something wrong and limped around for days with lower back pain. Often we are able to connect tension or injury someplace in our body to a generalized "stress," but most of the time we look for a physical answer, such as sitting too long at our computer, rushing to complete a job, lifting something too heavy, or stumbling over a curb. Of course, there are genuine physical insults to the body that can result in such injuries and it would be foolish to ignore these reasons. However, repeated emotional insults, blows to self-esteem, rejection, desertion, loneliness, anger, and sadness, they all end up, even when we no longer remember them, in our connective tissue.

Ida Rolf

In the 1930s Ida Rolf, a biochemist and physical therapist, developed a ten-step series of physical manipulations that she named Structural Integration. Structural Integration's purpose was to rebalance individual bodies by a unique kind of therapy. By the 1960s her method had become known by its now popular name, Rolfing. During the process of assisting people to bring their bodies back into alignment, helping them to learn new patterns of movement, the Rolf therapist presses deeply into the connective tissue, sometimes with the heel of the hand, sometimes with an elbow. Often, clients have found that pressure on these painful trigger points (points that coincide with acupuncture points that are along the meridians of the body, which lead directly to the

location of the chakras) brought powerful and unexpected emotional responses.

Memories of long-forgotten accidents, emotional traumas, and
other such painful past experiences and thoughts rose to the surface of their consciousness. Frequently, Rolfing clients have found
themselves awash in tears, not with the pain of the physical manipulation, but with the pain of the conscious recall of repressed
emotional experiences.

During the sixties and seventies a variety of Rolfers and other
movement specialists contributed to the evolution of what is now
known as the Rolfing Movement. It now includes a number of other
techniques such as Neuro Linguistic Programming, which encompasses individual counseling and problem solving to increase flexibility, and Aston Patterning, which is a process of gentle bodywork
and movement education to achieve physical alignment.

Mary Bond, in *Balancing Your Body,* writes that "When the emotional rug is pulled out from under us our response is just as real
as if the rug were real. When the earth moves, literally or figura-
tively, we temporarily defy gravity by buttressing the body with
tension. If this temporary bracing holds long after the fall, the body
accepts it as a permanent support, and the pattern is rigidified."

Be Your Own Biofeedback Machine

Biofeedback is a technique by which individuals monitor their own
body's stress and tension. Attached to monitoring instruments that
transfer muscle tension in particular areas into amplified signals,
the client learns to see or hear and to gauge and then adjust these
tensions. Research in this field has documented that the body and
mind are a continuum consisting of an intricate ebb and flow of
electromagnetic waves that can be changed.

It is possible to be your own biofeedback machine, without any
outside monitors, by being aware of the tension remaining in your
muscles even after a period of relaxation.

Put some music on your stereo that you enjoy, and you know
will relax you. You are going to check out your body for painful

trigger points that never seem to let go, no matter what you do, to discover if you are still holding on to memories that are painful. If that is the case, you are limiting your energy flow, keeping your chakras blocked, tilted or narrowed, and your aura weak.

A simple stretching and tension exercise will help you find some answers.

It is a well-documented fact that a muscle will relax more completely if you first tense it. Read through this process first and you will see that you are going to tense and release all the major muscles throughout your body in less than five minutes. You may already think you know how to relax, but actually it is difficult to do. We become accustomed to a certain state of tension so that such discomfort seems normal. Once a muscle becomes accustomed to that certain tension and a trigger point of localized pain or discomfort becomes the norm, it can be difficult to let it go.

- Set aside 10 or 15 minutes when you will not be interrupted. Go to a quiet place where there is no telephone or television and where no one will bother you. Lie on your back on the floor with your eyes closed. If you have developed a personal affirmation, repeat it softly in your mind so that you will close other thoughts out of your mind. Stretch out to your fullest, arms overhead, reaching and stretching. Take several deep breaths, listen to your breathing, and concentrate on how smooth and regular you can make it. Press your back into the floor. Now relax and let go of that stretch.
- Inhale deeply, tense and lift one leg a few inches off the floor, hold it there for a few seconds, and then let it drop to the ground as you exhale. Repeat with the other leg.
- Inhale deeply, tense and lift one arm a few inches off the floor, hold it there for a few seconds, and then let it drop to the ground as you exhale. Repeat with the other arm.
- Inhale deeply, tighten your buttocks, and raise your pelvis off the ground. Hold for a few seconds and then let it drop to the ground as you exhale.

- Inhale deeply, push your stomach out like a balloon, hold for a few seconds, and then relax those muscles as you exhale.
- Inhale deeply, take as much air into your lungs as you can, hold for a few seconds, and relax as you exhale.
- Inhale deeply, bring your shoulders up tightly to your ears, then forward in front of your chest. Drop your shoulders down toward your feet and relax as you exhale.
- Inhale deeply and squeeze all the muscles of your face together tightly, hold for a few seconds, and relax as you exhale.
- Inhale deeply, expanding your diaphragm, not your chest, relax and exhale.
- Inhale a little deeper, relax and exhale.
- Inhale again, this time a little deeper, relax and exhale.

Now slowly go over your body mentally, examine it, and see where you still feel tension. If you continue to have painful trigger points, be aware of them. This will give you feedback from your senses and your nervous system. You will be checking in on your attitudes and behaviors.

You may find that even after attempting to relax, there is an area sensitive to the touch or a muscle that still won't let go. Wherever the tension is located is usually related to the chakra that energizes that part of the body, and the result is that the aura is constricted or lacking in color. For example, if you find that there is a tender spot in your shoulder, you may want to do the work for the heart chakra again to uncover more ways that you can be more open. This self-biofeedback session will help you release this tension, as well as bring to your consciousness the need to find a new way of viewing how available you are to others.

This type of relaxation should be done often and with practice you will be able to speed up the process. You may find that you have unusual emotional reactions during these relaxation sessions; that is an indication that there are still emotional issues embedded in your muscle memory that need work. Periodically checking these little muscle memories can bring unconscious material to your conscious mind and help you to keep your aura shining brightly, with its full expression of the true and beautifully developing you.

Jan

Jan, a high school biology teacher, became interested in chakras and auras after reading about them in a physics journal that was lying on a table in the teacher's lounge.

"I'm a strange combination of a serious scientist and an individual interested in other dimensions and theories about the way the world works that don't seem to have any proof. I've read a lot about Zen and I often quote Robert Pirsig, the author of *Zen and the Art of Motorcycle Maintenance.* He said, 'The Buddha resides quite as comfortably in the circuits of a digital computer or the gears of a cycle transmission as he does at the top of a mountain or in the petals of a flower.' I like that because to me it implies that you can look for help or enlightenment, or whatever you want to call it, almost anywhere. It is a lot easier looking into things that you have around you all the time, than going to an ashram in India or traveling to Tibet, or trying to visit with the exiled Dali Lama. Learning something that might be helpful on how to improve myself or change my life came to me in that journal article, which mysteriously and serendipitously was left where I might find it.

"I took that journal home with me that evening and read all about the auras and the different wavelengths of light, and it seemed to make sense to me. I was interested in seeing if I could connect with the creative energy of the universe, if it was possible to feel anything happening when I meditated and focused on the different chakras.

"I've practiced some Yoga, but I'm not very comfortable sitting in the lotus position, so I sat on a big cushion with my back against the wall in my living room. I loosened my clothing and let my arms lie comfortably at my side. On the opposite wall of my apartment I have a big photograph of a snowflake. Most people know that each one is actually a crystal of ice and that there are no two snowflakes that are alike, that each and every one is unique, and that each one is made up of an intricate geometrical design. I think we all learned that in some elementary school class on science.

"I'll bet that every school kid has cut one out of paper, too. You know, you fold a piece of paper into a small square, then cut into the edges and cut out a wedge in the middle, unfold it and voila! you have created your very own snowflake. I remember we used to do them after the first snow and then each one was pasted onto the classroom window. I used to look at them while the teacher talked and wonder how, if we all had the same scissors and pieces of paper, they could all look so different.

"If you examine anything in nature, whether it is a flower or a shell, you will find that they are all actually small geometrically balanced works of art. In the Eastern philosophies such geometrically balanced designs are thought to be symbolic of the structure of the universe. They call them mandalas. So every geometric structure in nature, such as the snowflake, is a mandala. I guess people a long time ago realized that they could be a focus for meditation. All you have to do is look at the geometric patterns of stained glass windows in cathedrals and churches to see one.

"Many people use such a geometric design as a focus for meditation because it actually confuses the verbal left side of the brain, which cannot deal very well with spatial relationships. I often focused on my big snowflake picture and it always helps me to unwind and feel calm after a difficult day. I sat there, focusing on the center of the snowflake, my mandala, in a relaxed manner. That is, not staring, but allowing my eyes to soften their focus, which allowed these visual patterns to shift. Used in this way, a mandala will center attention and allow the usual brain chattering to slow down. After about ten minutes I was feeling quite relaxed and very centered.

"I had memorized the seven chakras and the colors associated with them because I was interested in the physics of the color spectrum, so I didn't have to look them up as I worked. I closed my eyes and began with the color red for the root chakra. I visual-

MANDALA

ized pulling the energy up from the earth. I concentrated on feeling it enter through my feet, traveling up the veins of my legs and into the base of my spine. I spent quite a bit of time on this because I could actually feel the sensation of the energy and I felt a very definite tingling sensation at the base of my spine. I concentrated on that chakra, urging the energy that I felt there to make this chakra spin rapidly. Then I began making that color fade from a bright hot red to a lighter shade and then on into the next color in the spectrum, orange. I took this energy, which I now visualized as an orange ball pulsating with heat like a giant glowing sun, flow from my spine to my ovaries. When I stopped this energy at my ovaries, I felt as if one side was warmer than the other. I spent some time trying to balance that energy on both sides of my body before I moved on up to my navel, where the solar plexus chakra is located. I suddenly was aware of a bright yellow colored light against my eyelids and I realized that I was thinking of my bile ducts and my gallbladder.

"I stopped for a moment because I had read that in the ancient sources the chakras are not separated into bad or good. But these sources saw a basic distinction between those of the lower part and the upper part of the body. Because they represent a three-dimensional world and each one has a physical, emotional, and celestial component in addition to its own particular viewpoint, they divided the chakras into realms. The lower three represent mankind's world, the upper three represent God's world, and the fourth chakra, the solar plexus, is a transitional chakra, taking energy in both directions for the benefit of all the others.

"I stayed at the solar plexus chakra for a while, and I began to feel rather uneasy but I didn't know quite why. I felt I was learning something quite important about myself. Anyway, after several minutes I took the energy up to my heart chakra and tried to calm the heat I was feeling. As I concentrated on my heart chakra, I began to feel tears welling up in my eyes, which surprised me. I don't cry very often. I consider myself a tough, strong, self-reliant woman. I've lived alone for a lot of years and I have resigned myself to the idea that I will never get married. Although I'm only thirty, I guess I'm going to be that old maid schoolteacher everybody jokes about. I've made my students my children. I enjoy teaching, particularly when I get students in my class who are really motivated and interested in biology. Biology is a big word. Actually, it means the science of life. Zoology and botany and a lot of other areas are included in it, so if students have any interest at all, I can usually find a direction for them to pursue.

"After I thought I had gotten my emotions under control, I tried to take the energy up to my throat but I found that I was all choked up. Pretty soon I was crying, sobbing actually, although I couldn't tell you what it was all about. I was pretty shaken after this experience and I decided to stop right there.

"The next morning I sat in my office at school and thought about what had happened with my chakra experiment last night. Suddenly I became aware that I had been having a nagging little minor pain in my abdomen for a while, but I had been trying to ignore it. I decided I'd better get on the phone to my doctor and make an appointment. It turned out that I had to have my gallbladder removed, but that is only part of what happened. No, I didn't marry my doctor, but he has a physician's assistant, Gary, working in his office, who just turned out to be the man I thought I'd never find—compassionate, caring, and trustworthy. We've been dating seriously ever since I got better from my gall-bladder surgery.

"Gary and I have been working together on meditating on the chakras ever since I told him the story of how I came to make that appointment that brought us together. Gary is very interested in alternative care because lots of the patients are asking about it and going outside traditional medicine. We meditate together and then work on bringing the energy up through our bodies. It is a wonderful experience to join with someone in an energy transfer like this. It has brought us very close together and I think it is something we will continue to do as long as we find it beneficial.

"When I told Gary about the Biofeedback Machine exercises, he was very interested. He called his brother, who is a psychologist, and his brother thought the concept had a lot of merit. Gary finds he has a lot of tension in his neck and he has been doing the Biofeedback Machine exercise right before we work on the energy transfer. He says that the work he has done with it has made him realize that he is resentful of the people who come into the office. They think he is the doctor and then make some hurtful remark to him when they realize he is *just* the assistant. Gary is also a singer, and quite a good one, too, although he doesn't have the kind of a voice that you could make a popular career out of. It is a operatic voice. He doesn't have classical training but ought to be doing something with it. He has been working on his throat chakra because he knows that he should be letting his voice shine somewhere, maybe in a church choir. He wants to avoid saying something back to the patients who hurt his feelings because he realizes they are simply expressing their surprise.

"Both of us are interested in seeing what happens when we can actually feel the energy rising to the crowns of our heads. We are hoping we will have what some people might call a Zen moment, a feeling of spiritual electricity and perhaps have an instant when we leap into the future or to a distant galaxy. Wouldn't that be great?"

Minor Chakra Tasks

Place your hand on the blank page of a journal and write whatever comes to mind.

Get up at dawn and look at sky.

Go to a church other than your own, where you can listen to their choir and look at their stained glass windows for colorful mandalas.

Buy a mandala coloring book and share it with someone.

Spray your bed sheets with perfume.

Visualization

Close your eyes and see yourself standing straight and tall, allowing all the energy of your chakras to flow easily, one to another. Imagine that your muscles are flexible and pliable, that you can bend and stretch easily as you move about your daily tasks. See the places where you hold old traumas softening and releasing their pain.

Meditation and Affirmation

You can create a meditation that is unique to your painful memories, one that will allow you to move on, create new positive energy, and strengthen your ability to hold yourself upright with courage. Create an affirmation that will strengthen your positive thoughts for the future.

Meditation

"As I inhale, I breathe in energy that will release all my tensions. As I exhale, I let go of old hurts that keep me living in the past. I am able to move my life to a new and more fortunate place. My life is good and I am well."

Affirmation

"I choose to live a life that includes self-forgiveness."
"I chose to find a lover who believes there is a divine plan for us together."

Minor Chakras Future

You should check your trigger points frequently, because it is easy to slip back into old states of tension, reinforce old hurts and memories, and incorporate new ones into your connective tissue.

As you become stronger and release old memories, hurts, and sorrows, you will find that friends and lovers will join you and help you move to a better place. Look around you. They may be there already.

13 The New Message Your Healed Aura Sends: Mr. or Ms. Right Will Feel Your Good Vibrations

Ask, and it shall be given you;
seek, and you shall find;
knock, and it shall be opened unto you.

—Matthew 7:7

You are swimming in a sea of energy. You are bobbing around in it, you are formed by it, and you contribute to its form.

Your aura is your electromagnetic field, vibrational energy that is available to you from the powers of the universe and then generated within you by the spinning of your chakras, energy that you now send out again into the universe. It reports who you are and how you feel about yourself, about others, and about the world around you.

As you perform these exercises and tasks honestly, a breakthrough change will occur and you will begin to create a new aura. It may seem that all you are doing is answering some questions and performing some tasks, but actually you are altering your consciousness and that in turn is opening up the energy pathways through which the power of the universe can operate.

As you change, the universe changes. As your energy contributes to change, the universe becomes more cooperative and you become more conscious of who you are and where you are going.

Hopefully, you have not selected only sections of this book and then done only the work that focused on your pleasure chakra, your love chakra, or one of the others, to the exclusion of all the rest. Each chakra is only one component of a total energy system, and as such, chakras do not function all alone but as a part of the greater whole. Any blockage, tilting, diminution of one chakra, or an excessively open chakra will affect the energy flow of those chakras, which will affect all of the others, up and down your energy system.

As you have answered the questions, written the paragraphs that explained how you felt and behaved in the past, and what your expectations are for the future, you have undoubtedly seen, felt, and thought about things that you now realize created an aura that either brought Mr. or Ms. Wrong into your life or prevented Mr. or Ms. Right from arriving at your side.

As you work on yourself psychodynamically and spiritually, your aura changes. As it becomes balanced, your chakras become less obstructed, allowing more energy to flow freely in and out. As you grow in character and personality, you will automatically begin to have a more beautiful aura. Ideas and thoughts that you had that prevented your chakras from functioning fully are vanishing, allowing higher vibrations and brighter colors to appear in your auric energy field.

Your way of life will change as you realize you are unique in the universe. As you clear away your negative beliefs and behaviors, you will begin to affect those around you in a positive way—you will transform your energy. By clearing away the blockages in your chakras, you open the doors to happiness.

Perhaps you now realize that you selected a role model for your life without really knowing the truth about that individual and you have now selected someone more appropriate to your life to guide your behavior.

Perhaps you realize that you selected someone to have a relationship with because of his or her visual impact on you, someone you found physically attractive, rather than learning about that person's character and behavior. Now you know that you must look at character before appearance and you will delay a relationship until you can discover whether there is a real person underneath the alluring facade.

Perhaps you realize that you ended your past relationships because of variations on the same theme. Now you know what that is and you will alter that negative behavior before you begin any new relationship.

Perhaps you realize that you selected a fantasy person to have a relationship with. Now you know that you need to spend some time getting to know someone before beginning a relationship.

Perhaps you realize that you selected someone to fill in the gaps in your own personality. Now you are working on gaining those traits you lack before you begin another relationship.

Perhaps you realize that the standards of behavior that your parents provided were not always the best and so you are creating your own behavioral code for your future.

Perhaps you realize that you don't have strong and enduring relationships with friends and family to give you comfort in times of loneliness and stress, and you will to try to rekindle those friendships and relationships.

Perhaps you realize that you limited yourself in finding someone to love because of gender stereotypical behavioral expectations. Now you will broaden your ideas of what a man or a woman should be.

Perhaps you realize that you allowed peer pressure to help you form your behavior and goals. Now you will take a look at the values of these friends before you find yourself in situations that are not of your own choosing.

Perhaps you realize that you have indulged in negative thinking and self-pity. Now you will change all this with positive affirmations that will assist you to live affirmatively.

Perhaps you realize that your life has been out of balance. Now you are making changes that will make your life more joyous.

Perhaps you realize that some of your past relationships could have been avoided or improved if you had listened to your intuitive voice. Now you will pay attention to your intuition and increase your observational skills.

Perhaps you realize that you had no definite goals for your life and for what you expect from friends, lovers, and significant others. Now you will set some goals for yourself that are positive and honest.

Perhaps you realize that you allowed your values to be eroded. Now you will review your ethics, raise your standards, and expect those around you to measure up.

As you look at the past, it would be easy to let the heartbreaks and the disappointments make you hardened and cynical. You need to work at changing so that you are open to the promise that the universe can bring to you. Out there, in that vast sea of energy that energizes the chakras and is manifest in the aura that is the unique you, there is an abundant supply of guidance, if you will just let it to come to you.

As the people in your life come and go, those whom you love and those whom you couldn't love, be aware that if you want something good, the universe will bring it to you. It will send you new people and new dreams if you will allow it to happen.

Perhaps you realize that in any relationship that is going to be worthwhile and lasting, there are questions about it that should be asked.

Does this potential lover, friend, partner have:

Character	Self-respect
A conscience	Honesty
Integrity	Compassion
Moral values	Goals
Courage	Faith
Principles	Trustworthiness?

And, do you?

Human beings have the need to give and receive love; to feel that they belong and that they are significant; to feel secure, to explore, and to learn; and to create something that adds meaning to their lives. In those things you are no different from any other person on the planet. However, how you satisfy those needs and feelings may be very different from the next persons method. In order to change your energy, you may need to give a great deal of thought to the honesty of your beliefs, thoughts, and emotions. You cannot change the past, but the future is where you will spend the rest of your life. Changing requires a great deal of courage. Courage is good, change is good—when they produce personal growth.

Your aura is the result of your personal energy, generated by your thoughts, emotions, beliefs, and behaviors. When your heart is open and your spirit is alive, you become more sensitive to people, places, things, and their energies. Now that you have brought unconscious material to your conscious thoughts, you are well on the way to altering your aura, to making it better, more rounded and balanced, as a new way of thinking and believing begins.

As the energy flows in and out of your chakras and up and down the channel that connects them, you will experience changes. The emotional changes you will feel may be strong, or they may be subtle, like a warm gentle breeze blowing against your skin. You may be surprised at your own responses to these changes. Examine them, look at them, feel them, experience them.

Unless you are one of those rare people who is able to see auras, you won't observe the colors of your aura change and flare out with brightly colored energy, but you will know that you are surrounded with a new brilliant and beautiful aura, because your life will change. Positive people will suddenly appear in your life. Your aura will now report a new truth about you, because you are the creator of your future.

Open yourself to the power of the universe, because it is endlessly generous. Let its mighty energy ground you and open your heart. Begin to focus on positive thoughts about yourself, your future, and the people you are to love. As you work on yourself, you change the world.

BIBLIOGRAPHY

Achterberg, Jan. *Imagery and Healing: Shamanism & Modern Medicine.* Boston & London: New Science Library, 1985.

Al Huang, Chungliang, and Jerry Lynch. *Thinking Body, Dancing Mind.* Tao Sports. New York: Bantam Books, 1992.

Bagnall, O. *The Origins and Properties of the Human Aura.* New York: University Books, Inc., 1970.

Bailey, Alice A. *Esoteric Healing.* Albany, N.Y.: Lucis Trust Publishing Co., 1984.

Barnett, L. *The Universe and Dr. Einstein.* New York: Bantam Books, 1979.

Becker, R. O. *Cross Currents: The Promise of Electromedicine.* New York: Tarcher/Putnam, 1990.

Bentov, Itzhak. *Stalking the Wild Pendulum: On the Mechanics of Consciousness.* Rochester, Vt: Destiny Books, 1988.

Bohm, David. *Causality & Chance in Modern Physics.* Philadelphia: University of Pennsylvania Press, 1996.

———— . *Wholeness and the Implicate Order.* New York: Routledge, 1981.

Bond, Mary. *Balancing Your Body.* Rochester, Vt.: Healing Arts Press, 1993.

Boss, M. *The Analysis of Dreams.* New York: Philosophical Library, 1958.

Brugh, Joy. *Joy's Way.* Los Angeles: Jeremy P. Tarcher, Inc., 1979.

Bruyere, Rosalyn. *Wheels of Light.* New York: Simon & Schuster, 1994.

Brennan, Barbara. *Hands of Light.* New York: Pleiades Books, 1987.

Burr, H. S., and F. S. G. Northrop. "Evidence for the Existence of an Electrodynamic Field in the Living Organisms." *Proceedings of the National Academy of Sciences of the United States of America,* Vol. 24, 1939.

Campbell, Joseph. *The Power of Myth,* with Bill Moyers. New York: Doubleday, 1988.

Capra, Fritjof. *The Tao of Physics.* Berkeley, Calif.: Shambhala, 1975.

Carlson, Richard, and Benjamin Shield. *Healers on Healing.* Los Angeles, Calif.: Jeremy P. Tarcher, Inc. 1989.

Chopra, Deepak. *Quantum Healing.* New York: Bantam Books, 1989.

———. *Ageless Body, Timeless Mind.* New York: Harmony Books, 1993.

Cooper, Paulette, and Paul Noble. *The 100 Top Psychics in America.* New York: Simon & Schuster, Inc., 1996.

Crichton, Michael. *Jurassic Park.* New York: Random House, 1990.

Crompton, Paul. *Tai Chi.* New York: Macmillan, Inc., 1996.

Csikszentmihalyi, Mihaly. *Flow: The Psychology of Optimal Experience.* New York: Harper & Row Publishers, Inc., 1990.

———. *Creativity: Flow and the Psychology of Discovery and Invention.* New York: HarperCollins Pub., Inc., 1996.

Cushing, James T., and Ernan Mullin. *Philosophical Consequences of Quantum Theory: Reflections on Bell's Theorem.* South Bend, In.: University of Notre Dame Press, 1989.

DeBecker, Gavin. *The Gift of Fear: Survival Signals That Protect Us From Violence.* Boston: Little, Brown and Company, 1997.

Dossey, B., L. Keegan, C. E. Gkluzzeta, and L. G. Kolkmeir. *Holistic Nursing: A Handbook for Practice.* Rockville, Md.: Aspen Publishers, Inc., 1988.

Day, Laura. *Practical Intuition.* New York: Villard Books, 1996.

Duncan, Lois, and William Roll. *Psychic Connections: A Journey into the Mysterious World of Psi.* New York: Delacorte Press, 1995.

Dunne, J. W. *An Experiment With Time.* New York: Humanities Publishing, 1958.

Fulghum, Robert. *All I Really Need to Know I Learned in Kindergarten: Uncommon Thoughts on Common Things.* New York: Villard Books, 1988.

Faraday, Ann. *The Dream Game.* New York: Harper & Row, 1974.

Fein, Ellen, and Sherrie Schneider. *The Rules: Time-Tested Secrets for Capturing the Heart of Mr. Right.* New York: Warner Books, 1996.

Foundation for Inner Peace. *A Course in Miracles.* Tiburon, Calif.: Foundation, 1985.

Garfield, Patricia. *Creative Dreaming.* New York: Simon & Schuster, 1995.

Gerber, Richard. *Vibrational Medicine.* Santa Fe, N.M.: Bear & Co., 1988.

Geller, Uri. *Uri Geller's Mindpower Kit.* New York: Penguin Books, 1996.

Grad, B., R. F. Cadoret, and G. I. Paul. "An Unorthodox Method of Treatment of Wound Healing in Mice." *International Journal of Parapsychology* 3 (2) (1961): 5–19.

Gravelle, Karen, and Robert Rivlin. *Deciphering the Senses.* New York: Simon & Schuster, 1984.

Hastings, Arthur. *With the Tongues of Men and Angels: A Study of Channeling.* Cambridge, England: Cambridge University Press, 1991.

Hunt, Valerie. *Infinite Mind: The Science of Human Vibrations.* Malibu, Calif.: Malibu Publications, 1989.

James, William. *Pragmatism: A New Name for Old Ways of Thinking.* Cambridge: Harvard University Press, 1975.

Jamison, Kay Redfield. *An Unquiet Mind.* New York: Simon & Shuster, 1993.

Judith, Anodea. *Wheels of Life.* St. Paul, Minn.: Llewellyn Publications, 1997.

Jung, Carl G. *Man and His Symbols.* Garden City, N.J.: Doubleday & Company, 1969.

——— . *Memories, Dreams, Reflections.* New York: Random House, 1965.

Kovach, Sue. *Hidden Files—Law Enforcement's True Case Stories of the Unexplained and Paranormal.* Chicago: Contemporary Books, 1997.

Krieger, Dolores. *Therapeutic Touch: How to Use Your Hands to Help or to Heal.* Upper Saddle River, N.J.: Prentice-Hall, Inc., 1979.

——— . *Accepting Your Power to Heal: The Personal Practice of Therapeutic Touch.* Santa Fe, N.M.: Bear & Company Publishing, 1993.

——— . "The Relationship of Touch With Intent to Help or Heal Subject; In-Vivo Values: A Study of Personalized Interaction, in *Proceedings of the Ninth American Nurses' Association Nursing Research Conference.* Kansas City: American Nurses' Association, 1973.

——— . *Living the Therapeutic Touch.* New York: Dodd, Meade & Company, 1987.

Kunz, Dora, and S. Karagulla. *Chakras and the Human Energy Field.* Wheaton, Il.: Theosophical Society in America, 1989.

Le Shan, L. *The Medium, the Mystic, and the Physicist.* New York: Ballantine Books, 1966.

Luks, Allan. *The Healing Power of Doing Good.* New York: Random-Vallantine-Fawcett, 1991.

Lyons, Arthur. *The Blue Sense: Psychic Detectives and Crime.* New York: Mysterious Press, 1991.

MacLaine, Shirley. *Out on a Limb.* New York: Bantam Books, 1984.

Mann, W. E. *Orgone, Reich and Eros.* New York: Simon & Schuster, 1973.

McGee, Charles T., and Effie Poy Yew Chow. *Qigong: Miracle Healing From China.* Coeur d'Alene, Id.: Medipress, 1996.

McBride, Joseph. *Steven Spielberg: A Biography.* New York, Simon & Shuster, 1997.

Mercado, Walter. *Beyond the Horizon: Visions of the New Millennium.* New York: Warner Books, 1997.

Monroe, Robert A. *Journeys Out of the Body.* New York: Doubleday, 1977.

Morehouse, David. *Psychic Warrior: Inside the CIA's Stargate Program.* New York: St. Martin's Press, 1996.

Myer-Czetli, Nancy. *Silent Witness: The Story of a Psychic Detective.* New York: Coral Publishing Group, 1993.

Myss, Caroline, Ph.D. *Anatomy of the Spirit: The Seven Stages of Power and Healing.* New York: Harmony Books, 1996.

Nhat Hanh, Thich. *The Blooming of a Lotus: Guided Meditation Exercises for Healing and Transformation.* Boston: Beacon Press, 1993.

Ornish, Dean, M.D. *Love & Survival.* New York: HarperCollins, 1998.

Ostrander, Sheila, and Lynn Schroeder. *Psychic Discoveries Behind the Iron Curtain.* Englewood Cliffs, N.J.: Prentice-Hall, 1970.

Pearsall, Paul. *The Heart's Code.* New York: Broadway Books, 1998.

Penn, Nate, and Lawrence LaRose. *The Code: The Time-Tested Secrets for Getting What You Want From Women Without Marrying Them.* New York: Simon & Schuster, 1996.

Penfield, Wilder. *The Mystery of the Mind.* Princeton, N.J.: Princeton University Press, 1976.

Radin, Dean. *The Conscious Universe: The Scientific Truth of Psychic Phenomena.* New York: HarperCollins Publishers, Inc., 1997.

Randi, James. *Flim-Flam!: Psychics, ESP, Unicorns and Other Delusions.* Buffalo, N.Y.: Prometheus Books, 1982.

Rhine, L. *Hidden Channels of the Mind.* New York: William Sloan, 1961.

Sagan, Carl. *The Demon-Haunted World: Science as a Candle in the Dark.* New York: Ballentine Books, 1996.

Sark. *A Creative Companion: How to Free Your Creative Spirit.* Berkeley, Calif.: Celestial Arts, 1991.

Schlessinger, Dr. Laura. *The Ten Commandments.* New York: Harper Collins, 1998.

Sharamon, Shalila and Bodo J. Baginski. *The Chakra-Handbook.* Wilmot, Wis.: Lotus Light Publications, 1991.

Siegel, Bernie. *Love, Medicine and Miracles.* New York: Harper & Row, 1986.

Sinclair, Upton. *Mental Radio.* New York: TimeLife, 1991.

Sparks, Laurance. *Self-Hypnosis: A Conditioned Response Technique.* New York: Grune & Stratton, Inc., 1962.

Stekel, W. *The Interpretation of Dreams.* New York: Grosset and Dunlap, 1962.

Storr, Anthony. *Music and the Mind.* New York: Ballantine Books, 1992.

Sugrue, Thomas. *There Is a River: The Story of Edgar Cayce.* New York: Dell Publishing Co., Inc., 1945.

Swann, Ingo. *To Kiss Earth Goodbye.* New York: Dell, 1975.

Targ, Russell, and Keith Harary. *The Mind Race: Understanding and Using Psychic Abilities.* New York: Ballantine Books, 1984.

Tart, Charles T. *Open Mind, Discriminating Mind.* Chicago, Il.: University of Chicago Press, 1976.

Van de Castle, Robert, Ph.D. *Our Dreaming Mind.* New York: Random House, 1994.

White, John, and S. Krippner. *Future Science: Life Energies and the Physics of Paranormal Phenomena.* New York: Doubleday, 1977.

Wise, Anna. *The High-Performance Mind: Mastering Brainwaves for Insight, Healing and Creativity.* New York: Tarcher/Putnam Books, 1995.

Zdenek, Marilee. *The Right-Brain Experience: An Intimate Program to Free the Powers of Your Imagination.* New York: McGraw-Hill Book Co., 1983.

INDEX